PRAISE FOR
STARTUP GOLD MINE

"A really useful guide for startup founders and big company executives alike. Packed with practical steps and common mistakes, this book is one to read attentively and keep handy for future referencing."

—MARIA THOMAS,
former Etsy CEO, SmartThings CMO

"*The Startup Gold Mine* is THE playbook for getting your startup-corporate deals across the finish line. Every founder needs to read this!"

—JUSTIN MARES,
founder of Kettle & Fire, coauthor of *Traction*

"Over the last decade, big companies have completely changed their approach to innovation, with startups at the center of those efforts. The Fortune 500 are turning to startups for innovation across every facet of their business, ranging from marketing and sales to customer service and logistics. Gone are the days when 'no one ever got fired for buying IBM.'"

—DAVE KNOX,
author of *Predicting the Turn*,
cofounder of The Brandery, CMO of Rockfish

"A productive relationship with the right corporate partner can unlock years of growth for a startup. On the other hand, there are numerous pitfalls along the way that can have you running in circles. The principles in *The Startup Gold Mine* give founders the proper framework to navigate the startup-corporate intersection to get their deal done."

—SEAN AMMIRATI,
partner at Birchmere Ventures,
author of *The Science of Growth*

"*Giftology* will get you in the door. *The Startup Gold Mine* will help you close the deal. This is a must-read book for anyone selling into large organizations!"

—JOHN RUHLIN,
author of *Giftology*, founder
and CEO of the Ruhlin Group

"I've been working with startups in rapidly growing and evolving industries for over a decade. The principles Neil outlines in *The Startup Gold Mine* are spot on and essential reading for any founder looking to grow his or her business."

—CHRIS CHANEY,
founder, president, and owner,
Infinite Esports & Entertainment

"*The Startup Gold Mine* is enlightening, interesting, and pragmatic. I copied whole sections to relay to my team, and repeatedly had to pause to write notes to action for our own clients. Nearly every founder in the B2B software space has the tough decision of whether to sell to enterprise or smaller companies. *The Startup Gold Mine* is an indispensable manual for those in the decision phase and for those with a handful of deals."

—ISHVEEN ANAND,
founder of OpenSponsorship, Forbes 30 under 30

"Factual, informative, and full of useful sound bites startups need to know about when it comes to working with corporates."

—RUPA GANATRA,
founding partner of FUTR Group and FUTR Ventures

"We built a multimillion-dollar business with Fortune 500 customers by applying the thinking Soni has shared. Your product, pitch, and performance do not have to be perfect. But you must understand these principles to succeed with big enterprise."

—SEBASTIAN METTI,
cofounder of Resolute Innovation

THE
STARTUP
GOLD MINE

THE
STARTUP
GOLD MINE

How to Tap the Hidden

Innovation Agendas of Large Companies

to Fund and Grow Your Business

NEIL SONI

HarperCollins
Leadership

An Imprint of HarperCollins

Published by HarperCollins Leadership, an imprint of HarperCollins.

Book design by Elyse Strongin, Neuwirth & Associates.

978-0-8144-3988-3 (eBook)

Library of Congress Control Number: 2018954576

978-0-8144-3987-6

Printed in the United States of America
18 19 20 21 22 LSC 10 9 8 7 6 5 4 3 2 1

CONTENTS

PART 3

Creating a Better Corporate Innovation Ecosystem
for Everyone   137

FOREWORD

Being a founder of a startup is exciting. You have a lot of impact and control over things, including the team you build, the product you create, and the processes for your new business. However, there are many aspects of a startup that can be mystifying, especially to first-time founders. I covered one of these areas, financing your company, in my book *Venture Deals: Be Smarter Than Your Lawyer and Venture Capitalist*.

Recently, as large, established companies have recognized the importance of innovation, the relationship between startups and large companies has become more prevalent. While large companies are often acquiring startups to build innovative vectors in their business, these large companies are also investing in and partnering with startups to develop new areas of growth. Through this activity, large companies are increasingly looking to startups to fill gaps in their innovation pipelines. From the perspective of a large company, this makes complete sense: predicting which new technologies will catch on is a game better played by entrepreneurs and venture capitalists. Instead of trying to make bets on technology developed in-house, large companies are waiting to see what is gaining traction before making a play.

The fact that large companies are increasingly looking to work with startups is a blessing and a curse. On one hand, large companies have many things startups want—credibility, distribution, customers, resources, and cash. These elements are some of the missing pieces in the startup puzzle.

But there is a curse lurking among these incredible potential benefits. When trying to work with large companies, startups face many challenges. Navigating the relationship—and these challenges—in a productive manner requires threading a needle that is often unknown and hard to discover for many founders.

Large companies operate at an extremely slow pace when compared to startups. What a startup accomplishes in a week can take a large company months to engage with. Startups can make decisions by getting everyone in a room; large companies often have torturous and endless approval processes. Decision-making in a startup is usually streamlined and well understood. Navigating a large company can involve numerous people, including many whom a startup will never physically engage with. By chasing relationships with large companies, you run the risk of slowing down.

Assuming you successfully close a deal with a large company, you then run the risk of becoming a product-development shop for that company. It is natural for a founder to pay attention to what is bringing in revenue and what could potentially lead to an acquisition. But, if too much attention is given to the large company, a founder risks abandoning her larger vision in favor of what she is being asked to create by her corporate partner. And, while the project you are doing may be life and death for your company, the success of the project is likely irrelevant in the short term to your corporate partner.

When *Venture Deals* was first published, the primary value we were trying to deliver to startup founders was a complete and open approach to helping founders understand how to interact and work with venture capitalists. The book you're holding in your hands fulfills the same goal for startup founders looking to work with large companies. You'll learn many things, including how corporate employees are compensated, what you need to do to initiate and close an enterprise deal, and how to avoid the many pitfalls that await you along the way.

BRAD FELD
Aspen, Colorado, May 2018

THE
STARTUP
GOLD MINE

INTRODUCTION

The book you're about to read is the book I wish I had back when I started my first company. As a nineteen-year-old college student, I knew next to nothing about how large organizations operate, and the bits I thought I knew were just plain wrong. My company operated in the higher education industry and interacted with large organizations all the time, including public school systems, universities, and companies. Our success, or lack thereof, in these interactions would make or break the company.

Like most startup founders, I grappled with how to get our foot in the door with large organizations. Following advice that I found online and through mentors, I experimented with cold emails, asked around for introductions, and went to events in hopes of meeting relevant stakeholders. I quickly learned two things:

1. Getting your foot in the door is time-consuming but, ultimately, doable.
2. The real challenge is how to close a deal once you're in the door.

The second insight sent me down a rabbit hole for the next seven years.

It is no surprise that startup founders want to close deals with large companies over individual customers or small businesses. Large companies can pay vendors six, seven, and even eight figures per year, depending on what the vendor is doing for them. As enterprises get more involved with startups, there are also opportunities to work with them as investors. And finally, as we've all seen, startups can be acquired for billions of dollars by large enterprises.

In an era when the pace of technological change continues to increase at an unbounded pace, large companies are increasingly looking to startups as their outsourced R&D departments. There is an understanding among executives that startups can operate in territory that is difficult for large organizations. This understanding allows large companies to manage their relationships with startups in a portfolio manner, with stages that include partnering, investing, and acquiring. Interactions with large companies are becoming a standard part of the startup life cycle.

After my first startup (during which we worked with organizations like LinkedIn and the Gates Foundation) and a stint as head of growth for another startup, I joined The Estée Lauder Companies to help build the external innovation function. One of my top motivations when taking on this role was to finally understand, from the inside, how a large organization makes its decisions, who is involved, and why things take so long.

As every founder or salesperson experiences at some point in time, corporate time lines and decision-making processes can be baffling. Even when a deal makes perfect sense on paper, corporates insist on taking their sweet time, seemingly not understanding the adage that time is money. Even more worrying, they didn't seem to realize that startups are generally on a countdown clock. At some point, your burn rate will catch up with you and your bank account balance will hit zero.

After multiple years of working inside of a large company, my conclusions might come across as somewhat surprising. At the core, I believe that frustrations and delays experienced by both sides are fundamentally created by misunderstanding each other, and this leads to a breakdown of empathy. Unlike what some founders believe, I generally do not think there is maliciousness on the part of large companies, though there are exceptions to this rule. Most individuals within large companies are doing their best within the constraints and incentive structures that they have.

In fact, I believe that there is a way for founders and anyone trying to work with large companies to "hack" the process and increase their chances of success. I put "hack" in quotes because it's the same thing that allows you to work with anyone—empathy. As a startup founder, you need to understand what your corporate counterpart is urgently trying to solve for, what they are worried about, how they get rewarded, and what else they are dealing with. Without this understanding, you're going to struggle and your chances of success in closing a deal are slim. You will be essentially relying on luck.

With an understanding of what your corporate counterpart is going through, there are steps you can take that greatly increase your chances of success and speed up time lines. These steps will help you build relationships on a more solid foundation that pay dividends for years to come. This is the process we'll be exploring throughout this book.

My hope is that you, the reader, walk away with a process—or at the very minimum, an understanding—for how to get deals across the finish line with large companies. As someone who has been (and as of this writing, is currently) in your shoes, I know that shaving weeks or even months off the deal-closing process can literally be the difference between bankruptcy and thriving.

I also hope that individuals in large companies who are reading this book walk away with a stronger understanding of how crucial it is to remove roadblocks in the way for startups trying to work with you. In an environment where large companies are seemingly facing competitive threats on all sides, the best path to staying ahead of the curve is creating opportunities that allow you to work with disruptive startups in a mutually beneficial manner.

CHAPTER 1

WHAT IS CORPORATE INNOVATION, AND WHY SHOULD I CARE?

You're probably wondering what in the world "corporate innovation" means. On the face of it, corporate innovation sounds like a buzzword big companies use to sound like they are taking risks and developing next-generation technologies, all while pushing the same old products with new marketing. That is only half right.

Although it's true that much of what happens in innovation groups at large companies would qualify as *innovation theater*,[1] corporate innovators serve a useful purpose: to identify areas of overlooked opportunity and to find solutions for potential existential threats to the company's current business model. Let's focus on the existential-business-model threat for a minute.

At its core, a business exists to serve a specific customer need, whether that need is coffee, tires, flights, or anything else. That need is backed up by insights into consumer behavior and preferences—which, over time, become ingrained as assumptions. As these underlying assumptions change—whether because of technological shifts, regulatory changes, or even something as seemingly trivial as fashion trends—businesses have to adapt their offerings to continue serving their customers. Usually these assumptions change incrementally, and normal business structures and processes can handle the necessary adjustments. Sometimes, though, there are major shifts, things like the rise of the Internet or the proliferation of mobile devices, that dramatically alter underlying assumptions and qualify as existential threats. When these major shifts occur, previously successful companies can topple practically overnight. The larger business community and media often ignore this dark side of business history, but it needs to be studied in order to understand the purpose and necessity of corporate innovation.

Companies wisely pay a lot of attention to their competition, but the truth of the matter is that established companies such as Coca-Cola and Pepsi will never put each other out of business. The same goes for MillerCoors and Anheuser-Busch, and The Estée Lauder Companies and L'Oréal. The reason goes back to those underlying assumptions. These businesses are all built to respond to the same set of consumer behavior and preferences. Yes, competitors may incrementally shift their core strategies and take percentage points of market share from each other, but they are solving the same problems with very similar methodologies.

For this same reason, when there are major shifts in the underlying assumptions, entire industries can be equally unprepared to adapt to the new conditions on the ground. To illustrate this point, let's look at the favorite corporate innovation case study of Blockbuster. Back in the 1990s and 2000s, Blockbuster was the most popular way for someone to rent a movie and watch it at home (the consumer need). To capitalize on this consumer need and serve as many customers as possible, Blockbuster built more and more locations around the world and started selling ancillary products like candy and snacks. Along the way, other video-rental companies popped up to capitalize on the same consumer need and compete with Blockbuster. The largest of these many competitors was a company called Hollywood Video. As these companies competed with each other, they used tactics like pricing, movie selection, and location convenience to try to take market share from each other. But at the end of the day, they were locked into a sort of dynamic stalemate.

Then in 1998, a guy named Reed Hastings decided to cut the bricks-and-mortar element out of video rental and created something called Netflix, a direct-to-consumer method for renting movies. The underlying shift that allowed this to happen? The Internet.[2] Consumers could go to the Netflix website, select which movies they wanted to rent, and have those movies show up in their mailbox a few days later. When they were done, they sent the movies back to Netflix and received the next set of movies on their list. By offering a rental service through the Internet, Netflix was able to cut out many of the expenses in the Blockbuster/Hollywood video business model, such as retail employees and rent.[3]

You already know how this movie ends. Unable to adapt to changing consumer preferences, Hollywood Video and Blockbuster both went out of business—Hollywood Video in 2010 and Blockbuster in 2013. But let's rewind the tape[4] and see how these "incumbents" responded when Netflix had clearly started to make a dent in their market share.

In 2007, Blockbuster started its own digital distribution service to directly compete with Netflix. Let that sink in for a minute. Netflix was around for nine years before Blockbuster launched a similar service of its own. While some of that delay can be tied to corporate inefficiency, it can mostly be attributed to the fact that

Blockbuster was not built to be a mail-order or digital business. Its DNA, so to speak, was in renting movies to people at retail locations. When Blockbuster hired new corporate employees, it did so on the basis of how well that person could support their retail business. Blockbuster's knowledge base simply wasn't built to support a direct-to-consumer or Internet-based business model.

So, did Blockbuster eventually realize that they needed to shift business models in order to stay relevant? Quite simply, no. As late as 2007, the company was still staking its future on retail. It didn't know how to do anything else. At the time, Blockbuster CEO John Antioco was asked about the Netflix threat, and he said, "We have everything that Netflix has, plus the immediate gratification of never having to wait for a movie."

What Blockbuster had entirely missed was the underlying assumption shift. As consumers became more comfortable with the idea of buying things online and having them show up at their door, they correspondingly became less inclined to visit retailers. If you could rent *Fight Club* online and have it show up in two days, why would you get in your car, go to Blockbuster, find *Fight Club* on the shelf (no easy task), stand in line, and then drive home? This growing shift in how people wanted to buy their products and services was in direct opposition to Blockbuster's DNA as a retailer, and therefore a true existential threat to its organization. Traditional business units, such as marketing or accounting, aren't equipped (or incentivized) to look for and solve existential threats. This is precisely where a corporate innovation group might have come in handy for Blockbuster.

Netflix's online movie- and TV-streaming service was the final nail in the coffin for Blockbuster. Once streaming started, people didn't even have to wait two days to get their movie in the mail. They could get the immediate gratification that Blockbuster (and similar businesses) previously had a monopoly on, with the added convenience of never having to leave home.[5]

How did Blockbuster and their competitors not see this coming? In hindsight, it all looks so clear. In the moment, though, these things were far from obvious for many reasons, not the least of which was technical infrastructure. Remember, there was a time when the vast majority of us connected to the Internet via a dial-up connection. Downloading one song used to take fifteen minutes. Imagine trying to stream a movie on that type of connection.

Although none of us has the power to predict the future with 100 percent accuracy, one of the main purposes of a corporate innovation group is to help prepare the organization for situations where the underlying assumptions change and the entire business needs to adjust. This preparation can take a number of forms—from collaboration with—or investments in—outside startups, to internal startup-esque teams, and a whole lot more. Corporate innovation's track record is spotty at best, but there are instances where it has paid off big-time. We also need to be cognizant of the unheralded corporate innovators who prevent their companies from being disrupted by timely recognition and prevention of existential threats. While we pay special attention to the companies who failed to see major changes coming and collapsed, as well as the companies who spotted the changes and became major successes, we ignore the companies who manage to adapt just enough to maintain their status-quo position. They don't turn into major successes, but they aren't disrupted either. To use a war analogy: people celebrate the general who wins the war and denounce the general who loses the war, but nobody recognizes the general who prevents a war from happening in the first place.

New, disruptive startups are only one part of the corporate-innovation enigma. Large companies invest billions of dollars every year in research and development, in the hope of developing the next game-changing innovation. These R&D departments are staffed by some of the world's best scientists, who work with state-of-the-art equipment to study and create scientific breakthroughs that will power their company's next billion-dollar brand. Obviously, coming up with a novel scientific insight isn't simple, but let's assume that an R&D group succeeds in developing a breakthrough innovation. Great, right?

Unfortunately, this is where a concept known as the innovator's dilemma[6] decides to rain on the parade. By virtue of their size, large companies focus their efforts on major opportunities that can add significantly to their bottom line. To put it in context, a billion-dollar company isn't going to spend much effort on a project that's bringing in $25,000 per year. Like most potentially destructive things, this is a good policy in moderation. Employee bandwidth is limited, so priorities need to be set, and large companies logically prioritize the biggest opportunities in front of them. But this policy can become fatal in instances where an opportunity is misjudged and overlooked as "too small" but turns out to be a disruptive innovation. Disruptive ideas tend to create new markets (as opposed to taking advantage of existing ones) so any judgment of opportunity size is bound to be incorrect. This misjudgment is what leads great companies into the trap of ignoring a major, game-changing innovation that disrupts their entire industry. Going even further, sometimes companies invent a new technology that's so disruptive to their existing business model that they can't get themselves to launch it, even though they would have a monopoly. The innovator's dilemma can be seen in action by examining Kodak's troubled history with the digital camera.

In 1975, Steven Sasson, an engineer at Kodak, presented a hacked-together version of a digital camera. To be clear, this was the first digital camera ever created. And it was invented by Kodak. According to the *New York Times*:

> The final result was a Rube Goldberg device with a lens scavenged from a used Super-8 movie camera; a portable digital cassette recorder; 16 nickel cadmium batteries; an analog/digital converter; and several dozen circuits—all wired together on half a dozen circuit boards. . . .
>
> "It only took 50 milliseconds to capture the image, but it took 23 seconds to record it to the tape," Mr. Sasson said. "I'd pop the cassette tape out, hand it to my assistant and he put it in our playback unit. About 30 seconds later, up popped the 100 pixel by 100 pixel black and white image."[7]

This is the quintessential hacked-together prototype. Sasson used the parts he had available, the budget he had access to, and his own technical knowledge to answer a feasibility question: Is it possible to take and store a photo digitally? Sasson had shown without a doubt that the answer was yes. Sasson's digital camera admittedly was clunky, not user-friendly, and clearly not ready for prime time. But the point of a prototype is to show technical feasibility, not to create a finished product ready for consumers.

Showing technical feasibility turned out to be the easy part. As Sasson explained to the *New York Times*, although Kodak's R&D team allowed him to keep working on the project, they invested minimal resources in the technology because of their beliefs that "no one was complaining about prints" and "no one would ever want to look at their pictures on a television set." In spite of this uphill battle, in 1989 Sasson and Robert Hills, a colleague at Kodak, created the first digital single-lens reflex (DSLR) camera—not a prototype, but one that you and I would recognize. It even used a memory card to store the photos.

You know the rest of this story. Kodak used their technical superiority and first-to-market advantage to develop an unassailable digital camera business that became the envy of the world. Kodak's case study in successful corporate innovation became an example that was studied by innovators in business schools and corporations everywhere.

If only. Here's what actually happened: Kodak's marketing department decided that they couldn't take the digital camera to market.

This decision only makes sense when you know that, in 1989, Kodak made money on every part of the picture-taking and -viewing process: the camera, the film that stored pictures, the picture-development process . . . everything.[8] In fact, the bulk of Kodak's profit came from the steps after the picture was taken. People only bought their camera once, but they bought film and had to get it developed on a regular basis. The digital-camera invention would completely disrupt this business, and Kodak decided that was unacceptable to them.

The one (temporary) saving grace for Kodak was their decision to patent their digital-camera invention. Thanks to this patent, they could cash in to the tune of billions of dollars, which staved off the final day of reckoning for the once-great company. Unfortunately, Kodak's digital-camera patents expired in 2007, and they filed for bankruptcy a quick five years later, in 2012. While we can certainly argue that the Kodak outcome could have been worse if they hadn't had the patent, the truth of the matter is that it only delayed the inevitable. Once they opened Pandora's Box (the digital-camera invention), their old business model was finished.

Over the years, these examples of once-great companies like Blockbuster and Kodak have terrified Fortune 500 executives. Nobody wants to be the next behemoth added to the infamous Blockbuster category of failed companies. At the same time, the adoption cycle for new technologies and products seems to be speeding up, which means companies will have even less time to react to new threats than Kodak or Blockbuster did.

In response, companies have built corporate innovation functions, usually with some or all of the following mandates:

1. Identify and get ahead of any game-changing trends or assumption shifts.
2. Build new businesses in adjacent industries.
3. Find ways to invest in and partner with the best startups in their own industry, instead of being destroyed by them.

The corporate innovation function can be set up in a variety of ways. Some companies choose to create stand-alone corporate innovation departments, while others embed corporate innovation functions within existing business units. Each company sets this up slightly differently, according to their own industry, culture, management team, and need set.

Contrary to what it might look like, the decision by large companies to encourage corporate innovation is one of the best things to happen to the startup industry. Large companies with a clear commitment to corporate innovation have built structures that allow their employees to work directly with startups. And when I say "structures," you should know that I mean they usually have *money* set aside specifically to work with startups. To paraphrase Wu-Tang Clan's "C.R.E.A.M.": cash rules everything for startups.

Another thing large companies have in abundance is scale. To put this in perspective, note that, as of this writing, there are:

- 706 Sephora stores
- 24,464 Starbucks stores
- 1,803 Target stores
- 490 Apple stores

Imagine a startup partnering with even one of those companies and getting their product/technology into all their stores. They would immediately have scale that would have taken them years and a boatload of venture capital to reach on their own. A great example of this is Nest, a company that makes the first mainstream-accepted smart thermostat. Many of Nest's early employees were ex-Apple employees, including founder Tony Fadell (who was one of the original iPod designers). The close connection between the two companies naturally led to a sales partnership, which resulted in Nest thermostats being carried by Apple stores as soon as they launched in 2012. Of course, this all changed when Nest was acquired by Google, a major Apple competitor, for $3.2 billion in cash in 2014. Now Apple no longer carries the thermostats. There is little doubt that Nest's incredible two-year journey from launch to $3.2 billion acquisition was catalyzed by their sales-channel partnership with Apple.

Startups have another thing going for them these days that large companies are after: startups are cool. Thanks to television shows like *Shark Tank* and *Silicon Valley*, books like *The 4-Hour Workweek*, and movies like *The Social Network*, startups have entered the mainstream consciousness. Large companies, on the other hand, have mostly become the antithesis of cool. Hardly anyone admits to aspiring to a traditional nine-to-five job, with its steady paycheck, retirement plan, and health insurance. In addition, the Enron scandal, the Volkswagen emissions fraud, and the financial system's collapse in 2008–2009 destroyed trust by exposing the dodgy ethics in place at many large companies. The continued degradation of the environment at the hands of "big business" only adds to the distrust and wariness that consumers feel about large companies. Working with startups allows large companies to borrow some of their cool factor. Whether it's a content partnership that lets them share your company's blog posts on their Facebook page, a co-branded ad campaign, or even a store-within-a-store concept, large companies are looking for ways to borrow some of the "cool" that startups seem to have in abundance. Creative startup founders can use this large company desire to negotiate favorable-deal terms, additional revenue opportunities, free advertising, and a whole lot more.

Large companies aren't just after partnerships. Corporations are increasingly getting more involved in the investment side of the startup world as well. Since 2010, corporate venture capitalists (CVCs) have accounted for approximately 20 percent of all venture capital dollars. This is being done in both late-stage investing and early-stage investing. Large companies like Disney, Barclays, and even the Los Angeles Dodgers have launched startup accelerators to source and obtain a financial stake in the next generation of companies in their given industries. And of course, large companies are still in the business of acquiring potentially disruptive competitors, which is happening at an increased pace as winner-take-all effects become apparent in nearly every industry.

Understanding why corporate innovators exist and how they can be valuable to startups is pretty straightforward. Similarly, corporate innovators can make their lives a lot easier by working with startups instead of fighting them. With the obvious win-win relationship potential between corporations and startups, why is it that deals usually take twelve to twenty-four months to put together, if they come together at all?

The answer starts with understanding how big companies work, from the inside.

1

UNDERSTANDING THE MACHINE— HOW BIG COMPANIES WORK

CHAPTER 2

PEOPLE, RISK, AND INCENTIVES

How Decisions Are Made in the Corporate World

Go to any Fortune 500 company's "About Us" page and you'll see some kind of testament regarding the company's dedication to its employees. Try to put aside your cognitive dissonance as you remember that this company has blocked websites like Facebook and Gmail from those same employees' office computers because the company doesn't trust them to get their work done. Also try not to think about the fact that these very employees (and not senior management) will be the first to go as soon as there is stock-price turbulence. This dichotomy between what happens in tough times to senior management vs. mid-level employees is one of the root causes of bureaucracy in large organizations. If you're not familiar with bureaucracy, all you need to remember is CYA: Cover Your Ass. In large organizations, whether those are companies, governments, or nonprofits, bureaucracy is a human construction used to avoid making decisions, as well as to mitigate the risks of decisions that are made. Thanks to the incentive structures used by large organizations, there is a huge, unspoken incentive to not rock the boat. Individuals who tend to make a big splash tend not to last very long in the corporate environment (by choice or otherwise), so odds are that in your interactions with large companies, you'll be interacting with folks who are masters of bureaucracy. These individuals are great at postponing decisions for as long as possible, as well as mitigating any blame that might fall on them if a decision doesn't go as well as they had hoped. The difficulty for a startup is figuring out how, against the usual incentives, to get the corporate machine to act in their favor. The magic for making this happen starts with understanding the people behind the machine.

A company, even a large behemoth like Walmart or Apple, is just a collection of people brought together for the purpose of selling a product or service.[1] Like other large groups of people, each company develops a unique culture. Understanding a company's culture and the people behind it is incredibly important for startups hoping to work with large companies. It's just about impossible to navigate the bureaucracy without some understanding of how various groups are set up, who is incentivized to accomplish certain objectives, and, ultimately, how working with your startup can make a person or group look great to their boss. Because yes, when trying to sell to—or partner with—a large company, internal appearances are everything. A deal that makes tons of logical sense can get completely derailed if there isn't anyone inside the organization who "wins" by getting the deal across the finish line.

This means that when you're selling to a company, you're ultimately selling to the people within it, which is a key distinction that's often missed. Therefore, it's impossible to understand how to work with the corporate world if you don't understand the people and organizational structure that make up a company. Into the machine we go.

The People You Will Meet in Corporate

In the course of your interactions with large companies, you will meet a lot of people and need to get skilled at sorting out who will be helpful to your efforts and who will be a brick wall you'll need to run around. Here are the types of people you will meet in corporate:

Lifer

I used to be surprised when someone told me they'd been at Company X for thirty years. No longer. As much as the media enjoys telling us that the era of staying at one company for life is over, there are still many people in that position. For our purposes, the Lifer is usually not the right person to work with to get a deal done. There's a reason they've remained at the company through thick and thin. That reason is that they've become experts at the corporate-politics game. This means that they're good at not pushing the envelope too far, they always support senior management's goals, are great at leading or taking meetings, can avoid blame when things go wrong, and above all, are excellent at avoiding decisions that don't involve other scapegoats. This is not the person you want determining the fate of your deal. With the Lifer, all the incentives point to you being called into an endless series of meetings with a decision continually punted to next quarter or next fiscal year.

To be clear, there's nothing inherently wrong with the Lifer. Some of the best employees I have encountered at Estée Lauder have been at the company for longer than I've been alive. These employees know the culture inside and out; they've seen the company in an era when it was much, much smaller; and some of them even knew, or worked for, the founder. There's something magical about that. The major downside, however, is that they often fall prey to the "we've already tried that" syndrome that plagues so many companies. Innovation is a complicated matrix of technology, business model, and, most of all, timing. When something didn't work the first time, it doesn't mean the idea or approach was wrong. The timing could have just been wrong, the technology not quite up to par, or some other messy set of factors.

Very few "new" ideas are truly new, which unfortunately means that someone has pitched a similar idea to the company at some point in time. The trouble with the Lifer is that they've seen everything and, like most humans, they learn from their prior experiences. So when they sat in a pitch meeting twelve years ago with a similar company and saw their manager rejecting the concept, they learned that concepts like yours don't help them achieve their goal, which is really to look good to their boss. From the Lifer's frame of reference, your concept has already failed, so why risk any political capital by bringing it up with their boss?

Beyond the disheartening fact that the Lifer has seen everything, they are also the employee type that has shown the least propensity to shake things up. People who constantly rock the boat simply don't last thirty years in one place. They're bound to piss someone off, mess something up, or just get bored.

Avoid the Lifer if at all possible. If you can't avoid them, don't get too discouraged if they reject your company. More likely, you'll receive ambiguous answers from them; the Lifer isn't one to give a definitive "No." What's the point of that? The Lifer is the undisputed champion of saying, "Let's stay in touch," or, "Let's revisit this in six months."

One final note of encouragement for those interacting with Lifers: they are definitely worth staying in touch with. As explained earlier, the Lifer is elite at doing enough to stay in the good graces of their boss. If you catch the Lifer at a moment when they're in need of a win, you may unexpectedly be able to use the Lifer to get to a decision-maker.

Striver

Have you ever wondered what happens to the teacher's pet when they join the workforce? They turn into the Striver. The Striver's goal is to maximize credit, and they will do absolutely anything to make that happen. Work weekends? No problem. Stab colleagues in the back when things go wrong? Easy. Get good at sounding smart without really doing anything? Piece of cake. The good news for you is that if you can find a way to make the Striver look good and get a win, he or she will do anything to get a deal done. Use their ambition to your advantage.

Since you know the Striver is chasing credit, make sure you include them in every meeting—even after they move you up the food chain to the final decision-makers. A pro move here would be to thank the Striver when you're on the phone with their boss. Nothing will make them feel better and more willing to work hard for your deal than knowing they're getting the right compensation for their efforts: credit.

Remember, above anything else, working with your startup is the Striver's deal. They'll do all the heavy internal political lifting for you, but they need to clearly be made part of the "team." The Striver will usually take the lead on this. The best thing you can do is find a Striver and then arm them with everything they need to make the internal push: pitch decks, one-pager summaries, technical support, and anything else. Once they take the lead, give them what they need and let them work their magic.

Corporate Drone

When we hear about white-collar workers having their jobs automated in the future, I'm skeptical. Not because I'm super-impressed with the critical thinking skills of the typical office worker, but because I think many of these people are *already* robots. If you've ever had the misfortune of interacting with a Corporate Drone, you know exactly what I'm talking about. The Corporate Drone takes one look at anything that doesn't fit neatly into their existing job function and spits out an error code, which usually takes the form of a resounding and definitive "Not possible." Any attempt to argue with this is ineffective and will be shut down. Do yourself a favor and immediately run away if you come in contact with one of these drones. If you're really feeling bold, the best-case scenario for you here is to get an introduction from the corporate drone to someone who is more likely to work with you.

Startup Wannabe

As many of us in the startup world are (sometimes painfully) aware, startups are *cool* these days. Humans like being associated with things that are cool, and corporate employees are no different. The Startup Wannabe is someone, usually a young person, who is more embedded in the startup echo chamber than any actual startup founder. This person reads TechCrunch and the like on a daily basis, knows all about the companies in Y Combinator's latest cohort, and is perennially thinking about how to bring "startup culture" into their company. As a rule, you can be pretty confident that this person has never worked in a startup and never will, but they like imagining what their life would be like if they left corporate. The Startup Wannabe can be a super-valuable partner when trying to find an "in" with a company. They are eager to build their startup network and will view a meeting with you as an opportunity to get closer to the source of the constantly sought-after "innovation." It may even be worth playing hard-to-get with the Startup Wannabe to make them chase you. The trade-off with using the Startup Wannabe as your introduction to the company is that the person is likely to be too young to have any real power. Your goal for the introductory conversation should be to quickly figure out if he or she has any decision-making power. If not, politely ask for an introduction to their manager. Chances are, unless the manager is a Lifer, they'll want to help you. Bingo.

If their manager happens to be a Lifer, it could be worth politely mentioning this to the Startup Wannabe. You can use phrases like, "Your manager has accomplished some great things, but she doesn't quite move at *our pace.*" This puts the Startup Wannabe on your team. As a result, they may open up some back channels to you—individuals in other groups or departments who they know to be better at getting deals through the system.

So, while Startup Wannabes might not have much power themselves, they are great at getting your deal in front of the right people.

Startup Refugee

As large companies continue to invest in the never-ending innovation chase, they have begun recruiting talent from the startup world. Increasingly, former startup founders can be found in corporate roles. This is unfortunate for the former founders, who often are coming from startups that went out of business, or buyouts where the only people who got paid were investors, but it's great news for startups trying to work with large companies. These Startup Refugees are often planning on staying in their corporate roles for a year or two while they rebuild their finances and their résumés, and therefore are highly motivated to leave their mark in a relatively short period of time. As former founders (especially founders who were involved in sales), they're also used to dealing with immovable obstacles and will hustle their way through the internal politics. Best of all, these are some of the few employees in corporate who will empathize with the problems you're facing while trying to sell into a large company. The best thing to do when working with the Startup Refugee is to leave the BS at home and just be honest about the product, value proposition, pricing, and everything else. Chances are, they will see through any dishonest sales pitch anyway, so don't bother. The other great thing about the Startup Refugee is that their default operating speed is still on startup time, meaning they will move quickly. The downside to these otherwise helpful corporate employees is that they will be harsh judges of any incompetence shown in your sales pitch or follow-up process. Having previously been in your shoes, they'll resent having given you a path to a sale or partnership only to watch you fall flat on your face.

Generally, though, the increasing number of Startup Refugees in corporate is a great sign for startups trying to get deals done. Working with this type of person isn't possible in every company; but if the opportunity presents itself, pounce on it.

Incentives: Why It's Easier to Take Risks When You Have Everything to Gain

To illustrate how the incentive structure works in a corporate environment, I'm going to tell you a story about parents and children—and economics. Bear with me.

Children often have big dreams. Think back to when you were a child who said you would be an NFL quarterback, a rapper, movie star, whatever. Then think back to your parents' reaction. Invariably, you were urged to be more realistic, right? It's true in even less-extreme examples. Think of the college kid who wants to drop out of school to build a startup. The parents, meanwhile, are urging their child to get a STEM degree and a steady paycheck, working for Oracle or General Electric.

So why are your parents always so conservative? As the wise philosopher Will Smith once mused, do parents just not understand? The answer can be found in studying economics and risk. Parents, whether they admit it or not, are protecting their downside risk. Think about it: If you don't turn out to be the next Drake, what's your next step? Go back home and mooch off your parents. Even worse, your parents face the painful social downside of telling their friends, family, and acquaintances that you're a failure and a bum—and ultimately, *they* are viewed as failures for *raising* a failure. People might not say that to their face, but social shame is real.

Okay, so that's the downside for parents. What's the upside? Not much. They mainly get to say that they are the mom or dad of [insert celebrity here]. Do you know who Taylor Swift's mom is? I didn't think so. There's none of the flash, pride, and satisfaction inherent in a self-made success. That doesn't mean parents aren't happy when you succeed, but it does mean that the *magnitude* of their happiness is similar whether you succeed in becoming a doctor or a rock star.

For the children, the equation is the exact opposite. The upside of an outlier success for the individual experiencing it is essentially limitless—money, fame, fortune, etc. What's the downside of failure? Going from poor college student to sleeping on mom's couch. Not a big change. You also get to tell your friends you failed at something pretty cool (like being in a band). Not the end of the world, and it may even get you some street cred.

Corporate innovation incentives vs. startup incentives almost perfectly map the parents-and-children situation. Corporate innovators have virtually zero upside for turning a project into a huge win for the company. They might get a promotion a couple months early (don't count on it), a small bonus, or most likely a plaque to put on their Open Office Plan Cubicle. If the project instead falls flat on its face, they have the downside risk of being branded a failure, since a failed project absolutely needs to have a scapegoat. There's nothing worse. So it's almost all downside for corporate risk-taking, as long as corporations continue to brand leaders of failed projects as permanent failures.

To be fair, in recent years there has been increased talk of accepting failed corporate projects as a cost of doing innovation. This is certainly a positive development, but we'll see if the talk is backed up by action.[2] A more motivational incentive structure could be to give employees some upside in the projects they create, because creating something from nothing is really, really difficult. Who is going to slog nights and weekends for three years, only to earn a plaque if they succeed? But my suggestion (hallucination?) about an alternative corporate incentive structure is just a pipe dream, primarily because in a corporate environment, compensation is used less as a true barometer of value and performance, and more as a way to indicate and confer status. It goes without saying that the CEO of a big corporation will be the highest-paid person in the company, and that salaries will decrease the farther down the ladder someone is from the CEO. The next factor used to determine salary is seniority. An employee who has been with the company for twenty years (hello, Lifer) will be paid more than someone in the same role who has been there for only two years. Allowing employees to have upside in startup-esque projects could open the door to shaking up the existing compensation scheme. In my imaginary universe of performance-based compensation schemes in a traditional corporate environment, it is plausible that a junior-level employee could invent a brilliant concept that leads to an entirely new business unit and millions of dollars of incremental revenue for their company. If that employee were given a percentage of the profits, it would turn the company's compensation scheme upside down, with more senior employees getting worked up about the junior employee's "unfair" compensation. Don't worry, this scenario is extremely unlikely to happen.

What is more likely is that large companies will continue to need startups to be the disruptive innovators, precisely because that's what corporate compensation schemes are forcing. Working with external startups is a way for companies to outsource the messy innovation work without shaking up their existing structure. Does it end up costing them a little more? Sure, but what's money got to do with anything?

Startup founders and employees have the reverse risk profile of corporate employees. Startups, especially at the beginning, have nothing to lose, so there is no downside. If they fail, no one brands them a failure; the founders will just move on to the next idea, pivot on their existing idea, go join another founder's startup, or, if all else fails, go join a corporate innovation department. (Just kidding, of course. Sort of.) In fact, with the increasing prevalence of the "cult of failure," failure has become a rite of passage and a badge of honor. And if the startup founders succeed, they obviously participate in the huge upside of a startup acquisition, IPO, or successful business. With these kinds of success-and-failure dynamics in the startup world, there's all the incentive in the world to go for it and try to do something big.

As the disparity in the incentive culture between corporate and startups illustrates, there's no mystery involved in understanding why startups do a much better job of driving innovation. They simply have a reason to try, and no reason not to. Employees of large corporations have almost no reason to try to radically innovate, and every reason not to. The innovation gap between the two types of organizations will remain as wide as it is today until either a) the incentive structure is fixed in corporate, or b) large companies realize the shortcomings in their incentive structure to drive innovation internally and create easier ways for their employees to solve problems and launch new products by working with external startups.

Credit and Blame: The Carrot and Stick of the Corporate World

Because of the weird, slightly perverted incentives in corporate environments, there's a lot of—let's call it "creative maneuvering" around who takes the blame for failures and the credit for successful projects. At the beginning of any project that challenges the status quo, there is a rush to see who can get as far away from the project as possible. This is understandable, since nine times out of ten, management will change their minds about priorities before the project gets off the ground. Why would a corporate employee bother wasting their time on a project that will just get shut down before any work is due? This is why it's of the utmost importance to maintain momentum in your conversations with large companies. Maintaining momentum includes things like press attention, new accounts (particularly if those new accounts are in the same industry as the company you're speaking with), and new product features.

The danger of losing momentum is getting pegged as a failing or stalled project by the corporate employees working on it. Once that happens, it's going to take a major event to get the momentum back. If a collaboration with your startup is seen as failing, you will begin to witness a whole suite of strategies that corporate employees use to stall, get away from, or deflect blame, including:

- *Blaming the vendor:* This is almost foolproof. People complain about vendors all the time, so it's easy for someone's coworkers to believe a vendor didn't follow through on something they promised. Part of the blame here goes to vendors. Vendors, which include startups, must stop overpromising and underdelivering.

- *Making a beautiful PowerPoint:* While a startup will likely never see the internal presentations or discussions going on behind the scenes, these meetings either drive momentum for your deal or stop any progress in its tracks. It's amazing how far a well-designed deck will go toward changing the perception of a project. The best PowerPoint presentation can mesmerize the audience, use all the right buzzwords, and, most importantly, obscure results, often using charts and graphs so advanced that they would confuse statisticians. A skilled corporate employee can use this technique for months to make a failing or stalled project be perceived as a winner.

- *Persuading someone else to take on the project:* The goal for a corporate employee here is to convince someone that they're doing them a favor by turning over the project. The double benefit of this approach is that if their colleague is able to turn the project around, they'll still get some credit for the win *and* the eternal gratitude of that coworker.

- *Winning:* Blame avoidance is only half the game. The other thing corporate employees quickly learn is how to latch on to a project that ends up having the perception of being successful. I once witnessed a unique technology development project in corporate R&D end up being moderately successful. During the development process, there were only five core team members on this project—each of whom had to fight to be given permission to work on it. The team members spent (uncompensated) nights and weekends working to validate the technology and the market need. When it was launched in corporate record-breaking time (eleven months), it created quite a buzz in the cosmetics industry but drove very little revenue. (There's that perception of success.) Once the buzz started, the speed with which other employees tried to join the team was remarkable. There were offers to present the project to management, contribute budget, and share technical expertise. Why the huge change in attitude after the technology was launched? All the risk was gone. It was all upside.

One final note on blame and credit: I'm not trying to suggest that corporate employees spend all day hatching nefarious schemes to steal credit and avoid blame. Rather, these examples are meant to show the behaviors and "skills" that employees are incentivized to learn, based on the compensation structures and culture in the corporate world.

How to Get a Corporate Promotion

Ultimately, human beings (and all creatures, for that matter) respond to the incentives in their environment. A startup founder chases customers because having customers means money, and money equals survival. In a corporate environment, the key incentives are promotions and, to a lesser extent, raises. The behavior you'll observe when interacting with corporate employees will make the most sense when viewed through that lens.

The behaviors that are encouraged by actions (promotions and raises) are often drastically different than the behaviors praised verbally by management. A great example of this is the corporate attitude toward failure and risk. Many corporate leaders today pay lip service to the "move fast and break things" attitude that's particularly popular in Silicon Valley. However, a company's actions betray its true feelings about breaking things. When someone gets branded a failure for a single unsuccessful project, there are greater consequences than that employee's career. People are smart. When they witness someone take an approach that results in a negative consequence (no raise and no promotion), they'll be sure to avoid taking that risky path in the future. This is what people mean when they use the term *organizational memory*. Employees remember when their colleagues were rewarded or skewered for doing things a certain way, and those memories get shared as anecdotes with new employees who in turn share them with the next batch of employees. This process repeats itself until the events, good or bad, become part of the company mythology. Thanks to organizational memory, each time someone gets punished for trying to break the mold, the "go along to get along" mentality is further reinforced and becomes even harder to shake.

The path to corporate advancement is ultimately about perception and risk management. Yes, advancement does have an element of competence involved, but that's true only so far as it falls under perception and risk management. If someone is incompetent, others in the organization will eventually find them out. Given the time lines involved (often two or more years between promotions), advancement up the corporate ladder is more of a marathon than a sprint. The fact that corporate employees are focused on how their actions are perceived is one of the biggest advantages startups have in their quest to sell to—or partner with—large organizations.

Let's face it: being innovative is perceived as cool. A corporate employee who finds or comes up with cool innovative ideas that *actually work* is going to drive conversation and make their boss look good, both things that fuel the perception that they are a valuable member of the organization who deserves to get promoted. On the flip side, trying ideas that end up failing will drive the wrong type of gossip and brand them as "reckless."

As we know, innovation is a risky business with lots of failure involved. How can a startup trying to work with a large company manage this apparent irreconcilable dichotomy between innovation and risk? The answer lies in taking something innovative and finding a way to reduce the risk as much as possible.

Innovating for Customers . . . or Managers?

For people who have spent their entire lives in startup culture, it's hard to grasp the true extent of how much politics shapes the day-to-day decision-making of large companies. Startups are largely egalitarian cultures. No one thinks twice about talking to the CEO or a VP, and likewise, most (unfortunately not all)

CEOs at startups are fairly open to taking advice from anyone in the organization, since you never know where the good ideas will come from.

Large companies don't operate this way. Each company is different, but there are politics in every large company, even the ones that were startups not too long ago, as Antonio García Martínez shared in *Chaos Monkeys* about his time at Facebook. Employees at Facebook were more concerned about coming up with ideas that pleased CEO Mark Zuckerberg than they were about creating new features for their users. In Facebook's case, they're lucky that Zuck has such a strong feel for the user that designing for him is not too different than designing for the customer. We saw a similar dynamic with Microsoft and Bill Gates, and Apple and Steve Jobs (and are currently seeing what happens after those dynamic founders leave). Unfortunately, most of corporate America's CEOs are not the original founders of their companies. Most are at best lifelong employees, and at worst professional CEOs who are world-class at managing existing businesses, but not so great (or even complete novices) at creating new ones. When internal innovators in any department start developing new products and solutions with their management in mind rather than their customers, it leads to major flops. This is the danger of using politics to drive innovation and why it almost never works. In fact, some of the biggest flops in corporate innovation history were driven by this designing-for-management dynamic, such as Crystal Pepsi and Google Plus. Unfortunately, this tendency to design for management and not the customer goes all the way up and down the org chart.[3] Think about it: an employee at a large corporation rarely, if ever, is able to witness the impact of their work on a customer. There are too many layers and groups involved in putting together a final product, which becomes truer as companies grow and departments specialize. So the only way for an employee to judge the quality of their work is by the reaction of their manager and other people higher up the ladder. This distorted feedback loop is yet another advantage that startups have over large organizations. Startups (again, generally) have fewer layers between the people interacting with customers and the product feature decision-makers.

Conclusion and What's Next

Understanding the incentive structures of corporate employees is essential to surviving the grueling process of selling to or partnering with a large company. The next step is understanding the corporate absurdities that employees have to deal with on a daily basis. While these absurdities will make you grateful for being in the startup world, you'll need to understand them if you want to do something as seemingly simple as scheduling a meeting with a decision-maker (welcome to Calendar Tetris) or survive a twenty-person conference call. Let's go see how the other side lives.

CHAPTER 3

INTERNAL CORPORATE ABSURDITIES

Day-to-Day Life in Corporate, and Why Startups Must Understand This to Succeed

Similar to how anthropologists study the lives of ancient civilizations to glean insights on their cultures, I'm going to take you on a tour of the corporate pyramids (so to speak) and share some of the cultural quirks unique to large organizations. My hope is that by sharing these quirks, I'll be able to give you some insights into how large companies operate and, in turn, enable you to better connect with them. Once you know what your corporate counterpart is dealing with, you'll be more empathetic to the sometimes-frustrating nature of trying to put a deal together with a large company.

Let's dive in.

Titles: A Uniquely Corporate Form of Compensation

Titles take on an overinflated importance in large organizations, as they are the only way to publicly show who is who, and for the leaders to reinforce their dominance. One example of the importance of titles is the practice of some large companies to prohibit their employees from emailing someone more than one level above them. I know it sounds absurd, but ask around: chances are you know someone who works at a company like this.

Titles are crucial when it comes to evaluating the "quality" of ideas and proposals. Ideas are never independent of their messenger, and this couldn't be truer in a corporate environment. An idea suggested by an entry-level analyst could be ridiculed as "outlandish" and "silly Millennial talk"; but when shared by an SVP, the very same idea becomes "visionary" and "disruptive." So goes human nature.

This is an important cultural quirk to keep in mind throughout all your interactions with large companies but is particularly relevant when prospecting and/or trying to move a deal across a finish line. Support from a high-ranking employee can take a deal from stuck to closed with a simple email. Cultivate relationships with those at the top of the corporate pyramid and it will pay off in spades.

Meetings: The Bermuda Triangle of Time

Meetings are like the Nickelback of the corporate world: nobody seems to like them, but they somehow manage to stick around.

Let me start this off by saying that, when used correctly, meetings are incredibly useful tools for making decisions, hearing alternative viewpoints, and identifying potential roadblocks. When used incorrectly, however, meetings will waste years of your life. If you've ever tried to schedule a meeting with someone in corporate and they've told you their "schedule is packed," this section will tell you exactly what they're up to and why it's harder to get on their calendar than it is to meet with the president of the United States.

Calendar Tetris: The Agony of Scheduling Meetings

How I envy you if the pain of scheduling meetings is something you are unfamiliar with. Here's how it works and why it's so difficult to get anything scheduled: when only two people are trying to find a meeting time, it isn't much of an issue. After all, I'm sure these two people have *at least one* opening that matches up, right? Now add a third person into the mix. Person A has three time slots available, Person B has three slots open, two of which match with Person A, and Person C has four slots open but only one of them matches with Person A and Person B. So there's really only one option for scheduling this meeting between Persons A, B, and C.

You can start to see how things will spiral out of control as you add more people to the equation. Imagine having Persons D, E, F, and G and having to match their time slots with A, B, and C. I'm getting a headache just thinking about it.

Scheduling a meeting with ten people is a form of calendar Tetris. May the odds be ever in your favor.[1]

In all seriousness, if you're trying to schedule a meeting with a large company, here are some tactics to use to reduce the difficulty:

- *Aim to have as few attendees as possible.* In this case, more is simply not better. In fact, it's worse. A lot worse. For each person you try to add to your meeting, you'll add a day to your scheduling time. In fact, let me turn that into a formal rule.[2]

- *Figure out who the key decision-maker at the meeting is and make sure they attend.* Once you know who the key decision-maker is for a given meeting, everyone else becomes a "nice to have" addition. Don't be rude about it, but once the key stakeholder is in for a particular day and time, make sure the meeting happens at that time.

- *Don't schedule meetings for Friday afternoon.* Nobody in corporate wants to take a meeting on a Friday afternoon.[3] Even if the other party agrees to a meeting, you're probably starting off on the wrong foot.

Meeting Calculus

Here's a little math problem for you: If there are ten people in a one-hour meeting and the average hourly cost per person is $100, how much does the meeting cost? If you answered $1,000, congratulations for knowing how to multiply. Joking aside, it's mind-boggling that companies who won't let employees expense a cab ride without eight pages of documentation can somehow allow just about anyone in the company to call a one-hour meeting that costs them four or even five figures in time costs.

This dollar figure doesn't even include the attention cost of a meeting. As Cal Newport so well describes in *Deep Work*, producing high-quality work requires long periods of work time without interruption. When your work time is interrupted by a meeting, it's not like you can immediately jump back into what you were doing before at full speed. You need some time to get back into the flow. Let's tentatively say each person needs thirty minutes to get back in the zone. The ten-person-meeting example above now costs the company $1,500. Ask yourself: Does this *really* need a meeting, or can email get the job done? And if a meeting is necessary, do all ten people need to be there?

But the figure above is just the tip of the iceberg, because we're assuming the meeting doesn't require any travel time or travel expenses. The only way that's true is if the meeting is a conference call (more on that below). Large companies, more often than not, have global operations and many times insist on key decisions being made at in-person meetings. This obviously requires travel. If the travel involves an international flight, many companies allow their employees to fly business or first class. These tickets can add up to several thousand dollars each way. For out-of-town meeting attendees, it's safe to assume a $20–$25K cost of attendance, including travel and time cost. There are some strategy meetings with twenty or more attendees, most of them from out of town. While setting corporate strategy for a multibillion-dollar company is arguably worth a couple million dollars in travel expenses, I guarantee companies aren't thinking about these things in clear, explicit terms like that, thanks to budget silos.

Conference Calls

As much as we rail against in-person meetings, the conference call is a far more common form of meeting in global organizations with offices spread out all over the world. The conference call is a particularly subtle time sink, partially because of how simple the invitation process is. After all, it only takes a couple more clicks to invite ten people to a call than five. And you don't even have to worry about meeting-room sizes and logistics.

If you've ever been part of a large conference call (more than five people normally qualifies), particularly an internal corporate meeting, you know that the meeting quickly ends up being the core group of people who needed to attend (usually three or four people) and silence from the rest of the crowd. Not coincidentally, being invited to a conference call but not having to participate is a great time to get actual work done, because your calendar is blocked off but you don't have to present or share anything.[4] On a related note, we all owe a great debt to whoever invented the mute button on phones. Thank you for your contribution to humanity.

For some reason that has been lost to the depths of history, conference calls can generally be found in two varieties: thirty minutes and one hour. Somehow, we corporate employees have figured out how to box any type of conversation into those standard time lengths. About a year into my corporate life, I started to question this assumption and examine the nature of conference calls. How come meetings only end late, never early? Why is it that we only seem to get to the business at hand toward the end of the call? Why do meetings always seem to generate more meetings?

What I found was that changing the length of time for meetings doesn't change what you accomplish in them. In fact, you sometimes get more accomplished because of the time pressure. I started by changing most meetings that otherwise would have been thirty minutes to twenty minutes and all one-hour meetings to forty-five minutes.[5] I'll admit that initially this move was not popular. Humans generally don't like it when someone rocks the boat, no matter how softly. But I soon started seeing others using the same tactic. I eventually started using fifteen minutes and forty minutes as my standard meeting lengths to try to shorten things further, with no negative consequences.

Formal In-Person Meetings

If you've never done a formal in-person meeting with a large corporation, it can be a weird experience. It certainly was strange for me when I went into my first corporate meetings as a college startup founder. There's a learning curve to the cadence of these meetings that can only be described as learning how to interact in a foreign culture. The tentative agenda of most of these meetings is as follows:

2:00 p.m.—Introductions: Each team will talk for a few minutes about who they are, their function, and their interest in the meeting/company/technology.

2:15 p.m.—The startup will be asked to share their deck (possibly for the tenth time, if there was already one or several phone meetings).

2:30 p.m.—There will be questions about the deck (which may have already been answered several times).

2:45 p.m.—You finally get to the agenda of the meeting, which is to discuss the potential relationship between your startup and the large corporation.

3:00 p.m.—Time runs out, and several of the attendees need to "run" to other meetings. You and the rest of the attendees agree to a follow-up meeting to get into more detail about the specifics of a partnership.

If this is your first time going through this process, you'll think you just wasted your time and money in taking an in-person meeting to get nothing accomplished. In fact, the opposite is true: you *nailed* the meeting. The purpose of this meeting was to get the corporate team you'll be working with comfortable with the idea of working with your company—and, just as important, comfortable with *you* as a founder. More on this later when we get into the specifics of how to get a deal done.

The Clock

The very idea of being an employee boils down to reliably pre-selling forty hours per week of your time in exchange for that awesome—yet addicting—opioid called a salary.

There's a saying among engineers that you may have heard before: "The best engineers are the lazy ones." The reason is that an engineer should be compensated for getting the job done and not for the amount of time spent on a project. Since the engineer is only focused on getting the job done correctly, they will naturally do the minimum work required to arrive at the desired outcome.

This idea doesn't only apply to engineers. Similarly, startup employees know that their companies only have a set amount of time before they run out of cash. This fact provides the "kick in the rear" to work on the right things and get them accomplished as quickly as possible. In Facebook's IPO letter, Mark Zuckerberg tells investors that Facebook favors a culture of iteration and continuous improvements by sharing that they have the phrase "Done is better than perfect"[6] painted on their walls. If there is a better phrase to exemplify the startup ethos, I haven't found it.

This same idea doesn't quite apply to corporate employees. In fact, the opposite dynamic is often at play. Since corporate employees have pre-sold their time, their incentive is for things to take as long as possible. And nothing takes longer than making something perfect. This is mostly not the fault of corporate employees. After all, a mature company is in the business of offering a product or service that's consistently great and, just as important, is homogenous. That means Coca-Cola has to taste the same whether you drink it at a restaurant in Miami or a roadside stand in Mumbai. MAC lipstick can't have a different texture every time you buy it. Bud Light has to have the same watery taste everywhere. As anyone who has ever tried to cook knows quite well, creating the same product time after time is much more difficult than it seems. There are so many variables that come into play with creating something as simple as a meal: quality of ingredients (not to mention the origin, growing conditions, and storage/transport of those ingredients), cooking equipment quality/cleanliness, ambient conditions, the chef's technique, and so much more. Now imagine scaling that up for a more complicated product, like a cancer drug. Ensuring consistency, quality, and safety is no small task, and it's one of the things large organizations do best. This is outside our current scope, but one thing that separates the wheat from the chaff when it comes to companies trying to scale is their ability to solve the issues of consistency and homogeneity in their product.

But regardless of how much skill it takes to make a consistent mass-scale product, that desire really gets in the way when it comes to innovation. The job of an innovator, whether they're in corporate or an independent entrepreneur, is to discover and home in on what people want through experimentation. Experimentation and, more importantly, iteration lend themselves to limited-time development cycles, minimal cash investment, and heaping amounts of user and customer feedback. Large corporations, by necessity, become really good at executing on an existing product, which requires none of the things experimentation does.

To put it another way, innovators take something from 0 percent product-market fit to 90 percent. This is what famed entrepreneur and investor Peter Thiel was referring to in the title of his brilliant book *Zero to One*. In contrast, large corporations and the people who work for them get really good at taking something that's at 90 percent and bringing it up to 99 percent. There are two very different skill sets involved here. Innovators would probably do a less-than-stellar job of taking something to 99 percent. Yet large corporations insist on taking people who have spent their life in the 90 to 99 percent range and putting them in corporate innovation roles that require 0 to 90 percent thinking.

Getting back to time scales: when it's done in a lean fashion, going from 0 to 90 percent can take an incredibly short amount of time. This could potentially be as short as a few months, and sometimes even less. It usually doesn't cost much money, either. Contrast that with the process required to take a product to consistent scale: there are safety concerns, logistics, regulatory mazes to navigate through, and a supply chain to create. These things are done on a time scale of *years*. Taking someone who is used to operating in a time frame measured in *years* and asking them to transition immediately to a weeks-or-days mind-set is asking for trouble.

Evolution and Corporate Instincts

Every large organization that's been around for any period of time develops processes, instincts, and organizational memory.

Most of that memory and instinct is beneficial and ensures the survival of the organization. It's akin to instincts in living organisms: our instincts have survived for the simple reason that they were passed on by our predecessors through the ages, and those predecessors were able to survive long enough to pass their genes on. Some of the beneficial instincts—the desire to mate, for example—help us pass our genes on to the next generation and ensure survival of our species.

Yet some of our instincts, such as the desire to consume as much sugar as possible, don't match our current environment. Two hundred thousand years ago, when an early human came across a beehive and had the opportunity for a sugar feast, there was a real survival benefit to gorging as much as possible since there was no way of knowing when he'd ever see sugar again. There was also a benefit for his body to store the caloric surplus as body fat. After all, the beehive wouldn't be there forever—and even if it would, the early human probably wouldn't. So he needed a way to take the beehive "to go." Fat storage was the most perfectly evolved solution to this problem in that early human's environment.

Today, however, we live in a very different environment. Sugar, at least in the First World, is the most abundant energy source, and we accordingly have diseases caused by excess sugar. Yet in spite of our conscious knowledge of the dangers of sugar, we continue to consume it in prodigious quantities, thanks to our instincts that tell us to leave no sugar calorie behind because WHO KNOWS WHEN WE'LL GET ANOTHER.

Similarly, large companies preserve and pass on many legacy instincts, most of which are useful and help the company survive. At any given time, however, there are processes that may have been helpful at some point in the company's history but are completely irrelevant or even harmful in the company's current operating environment. Corporate instincts, just like biological instincts, take time to adapt to new environments and many times result in extinction rather than adaptation—leaving a new, better-adapted company to survive in their absence.

A clear example of this that I encountered quite often during my time at Estée Lauder is the legacy distribution channel. Estée Lauder rose to prominence in large part thanks to figuring out how to leverage the department store. Macy's, Nordstrom, Bergdorf Goodman, and Bloomingdale's were major contributors to the success of The Estée Lauder Companies, and appropriately these stores were treated with respect and deference. There was clear logic to this: you don't want to piss off your largest sales channel. Over time, prioritizing department stores was built into the corporate culture, because those who did prioritize these stores were rewarded with better results and were promoted throughout the company.

However, at some point between the early 1990s and 2008, it became clear that this new thing called the Internet was going to drastically change the retail environment in a way that would reduce the market share of department stores. Contrary to what many in the startup community believe, brands (like Estée Lauder) that sell in department stores didn't have their head in the sand. There was widespread agreement and understanding that the distribution landscape was about to change for good. Where brands ran into trouble was in taking those insights and turning them into action, which would have required overriding their corporate instincts prioritizing department stores. Thanks to these legacy instincts, they were unable to convert these insights to action in the same way a lean, five-person startup might have taken advantage of them. While these legacy retail brands are better adapted to the Internet now than in the mid-2000s, they are still fighting an uphill battle against the instinctual drive to accommodate and prioritize department stores over other sales channels that may focus on e-commerce, mobile, or other direct-to-consumer methods.

Legacy instincts go far beyond distribution strategy. They affect everything from employee recruiting, organization structure, manufacturing/production, quality control, marketing, to even R&D. When (and it's truly a matter of when, not if) you run up against a process that seems absurd, understand that you're facing the product of a legacy corporate instinct.

Nim De Swardt, Chief Next Generation Officer at Bacardi, offered the following advice to Intrapreneurs, something founders should take note of as they approach corporate innovation groups:

You have to have faith in your capabilities to embrace constant change as an Intrapreneur. Business changes, leadership changes, societal changes, the changing consumer—unknown over known, wild over tame, change over constant, courage over comfort.

Corporate C Suites around the world face similar challenges. "Everything is all good" is a message that is constantly being projected to the top. What if we delivered honest introspection, front-line employee insights, and reframed our biggest challenges as our greatest opportunity? The new world of business and work needs to accept that they are now balancing a fine line between traditions and driving a new world change agenda.

You can read more about Nim's work and ideas in the Appendix.

"Innovative Office" Design

To an outsider, office design may seem like a strange thing to pick on. After all, nothing could be worse than the standard American cubicle, right? While I'm not claiming that the cubicle is a great boon for morale or productivity, the design of corporate-innovation offices seems to have been done without any regard for the actual people working in them.

If you've never seen a corporate-innovation office from the inside, let me describe it for you: imagine that someone in charge of deciding office layouts read those descriptions of Google/Facebook/Twitter's offices, or a description of most any startup office, and unilaterally decided, "We need that." Management can't help but think those descriptions sound pretty cool, with their open layouts, ping-pong tables, beer, and free snacks. So the decision is made that the innovation office will have a "startup feel," whatever that means, and the office is built—often at a multimillion-dollar cost. Once the office is opened with great fanfare, the grumbling and complaints start. Here's why people are complaining:

- **No More Corner Offices**

  Imagine if you'd worked for a company for twenty years and finally made it to VP. One of the perks is you've been given an escape from the cubicle life and now have your very own office. Now imagine that your office gets snatched away from you by the company's new Chief Innovation Officer, who says everyone is going to sit in an Open Office with no assigned desks. Not only do you not have a private office, you don't even have your cubicle anymore! And the icing on the cake is that your boss, an SVP, is exempt from this rule and still gets a private office. Fun, right?

- **Phone Calls**

  In startups, most meetings are done in person for the simple reason that everyone is (usually) sitting in the same room/floor/building. In large, global companies, many or most meetings are done by phone because of the distributed workforce spread out across the globe. In an open office, phone calls are a major liability. Not only is there no privacy, but there is also the added bonus of getting to disturb all your colleagues.

- **Constant Distractions**

  When everyone has access to everyone all the time, there's basically no barrier to interrupting, making it extremely difficult to get deep work done. On one hand, the increased collaboration is good and reduces information silos; but on the other hand, not having the ability to focus can't help but result in shallower insights, lower idea quality, and more politicking.

Innovation office layouts are another example of "innovation theater," yet another instance of large companies incentivizing the appearance of innovation over actual innovation. Obvious statement of the day: having an office that looks like Google's isn't the same thing as having an innovation culture on par with Google.

Administrative Assistants

I have a confession to make: my favorite people in the corporate world are administrative assistants (or "admins" for short). They are among the most intelligent, resourceful, and clever individuals within any company, and they have that rare ability to take shit from others with a smile on their face. Admins have helped me with plenty that I would've been completely out of luck with on my own, including but not limited to: IT issues, transportation in a snowstorm, parking, getting in contact with someone, nudging someone to make a decision, travel, and so much more. I haven't even mentioned that admins are by far the best Calendar Tetris players in the universe. Can't match up even three people's schedules and your boss asks you to help schedule a twenty-person meeting? I bet an admin can help. I'm also willing to bet that admins are among the top 10 percent most productive employees within any large company.

So to all the admins out there, keep doing what you do. The corporate world would fall apart without you. Seriously.

Now, that being said, there is one thing around the corporate culture of having admins that is annoying and counterproductive. It goes back to showing your status in the hierarchy. Having an admin is a sign that "you've made it" in corporate. You're important enough that you need someone screening your calls, scheduling your meetings, and helping you with paperwork. To be clear, there's absolutely nothing wrong with getting help to manage your schedule. The problems start when having that scheduling help becomes a proxy for status *and* that status is flaunted in the face of others, in the form of passive-aggressive emails saying "ask my admin."

If you're on the receiving end of the infamous, curt "ask my admin" email, know that it isn't a sign that the corporate innovator isn't interested in talking to you. It's their subtle way of showing off—what rappers call "flexing"—their superior status. Be polite to the admin—remember he or she is the real gatekeeper.

Information and Decision-Making Bottlenecks

The traditional corporate "org chart" looks a lot like a triangle with a wide base (entry-level employees) that narrows as it reaches the apex (the CEO). The org chart was invented in 1854 by Daniel McCallum, superintendent of the New York and Erie Rail Road, as a way of visualizing the structure of the company. Interestingly, while the org chart as it relates to companies came about in the nineteenth century, the structure itself dates back millennia to the Romans, who pioneered its use in a military hierarchy organization.

The org chart isn't inherently bad. After all, the CEO doesn't have the bandwidth to do double duty as a cashier. Where things get wacky is when we start talking about decision-making.

Most corporate leaders toe the party line when it comes to delegation. They've read several *Harvard Business Review* articles telling them how valuable it is to delegate responsibilities; they may even encourage their direct reports to delegate things to others. But as usually happens in the real world, people have trouble practicing what they preach. Despite all the talk about the importance of delegating, decisions tend to flow through one or two key individuals in each department, usually SVP-type folks who have the exclusive power to approve or deny any key actions, especially the ones that involve spending money.

To an extent, limiting who controls spending is a prudent measure. After all, maybe the entry-level employee isn't quite ready to make multimillion-dollar spending decisions. But when this is applied as a blanket rule, covering even small decisions, things start to get thrown out of whack. A Director or VP should have the ability to spend a couple hundred bucks at their discretion. If they can't even be trusted to do that, why were they hired in the first place?

Sometimes these bottlenecks have less to do with budgeting and more to do with scheduling. There are only eight hours in a typical workday, and if all decisions need to flow through one person, it may take a while to get on their calendar and make the case for why the funding should be approved. The decision-maker in this case is also arriving on the scene without any context, setting the stage for a bad decision—either in favor or against. This is the best case for decision-making delegation: the people with the facts are able to make the decision.

Tesla: A Case Study

Elon Musk has built an incredible company at Tesla. But even he is worried about corporate silos and information bottlenecks. In 2017, this company-wide internal Tesla email highlighting the information-flow problem was leaked:

> Subject: Communication Within Tesla
>
> There are two schools of thought about how information should flow within companies. By far the most common way is chain of command, which means that you always flow communication through your manager. The problem with this approach is that, while it serves to enhance the power of the manager, it fails to serve the company.
>
> Instead of a problem getting solved quickly, where a person in one dept talks to a person in another dept and makes the right thing happen, people are forced to talk to their manager who talks to their manager who talks to the manager in the other dept who talks to someone on his team. Then the info has to flow

back the other way again. This is incredibly dumb. Any manager who allows this to happen, let alone encourages it, will soon find themselves working at another company. No kidding.

Anyone at Tesla can and should email/talk to anyone else according to what they think is the fastest way to solve a problem for the benefit of the whole company. You can talk to your manager's manager without his permission, you can talk directly to a VP in another dept, you can talk to me, you can talk to anyone without anyone else's permission. Moreover, you should consider yourself obligated to do so until the right thing happens. The point here is not random chitchat, but rather ensuring that we execute ultra-fast and well. We obviously cannot compete with the big car companies in size, so we must do so with intelligence and agility.

One final point is that managers should work hard to ensure that they are not creating silos within the company that create an us vs. them mentality or impede communication in any way. This is unfortunately a natural tendency and needs to be actively fought. How can it possibly help Tesla for depts to erect barriers between themselves or see their success as relative within the company instead of collective? We are all in the same boat. Always view yourself as working for the good of the company and never your dept.

Thanks,

Elon

If Tesla, an organization that is more direct than most, can find themselves falling into this problem, so can any other large organization. As Musk alludes to, there is a natural tendency for humans in large groups to devolve into silos where information doesn't flow freely. Perhaps this is a legacy of our tribal background; but regardless of reason, it seems to be a naturally occurring phenomenon. This point is very important to understand. Large companies don't develop silos because they are "dumb," any more than people age because they are "dumb." Information silo development seems to be something akin to entropy—it just happens. And any desire to prevent it is going to require work and active effort.

As a side note, it's much easier for senior management within a company to see the silo phenomenon occurring than it is for individual department managers to see it. Department managers are usually judged (and given bonuses) based on the performance of their department rather than the entire company, so naturally their attention will be focused on the department's performance. Smart companies figure out ways around this by linking individual compensation to overall company performance, but silos will still occur. This is something senior management needs to actively work against, as Musk did in his email.

Once you have an understanding of this phenomenon, it's easier to be sympathetic to what your corporate counterpart is dealing with—and, if nothing else, it hopefully increases your patience with corporate time lines.

Optimizing for the Wrong Variables

When Peter Drucker said, "You can't manage what you can't measure," I don't *think* he wanted to create a Frankenstein.

Unfortunately, most of us humans are mindless automatons: when we're told to increase our email click-through rate or reduce the cost of a cosmetics package, we use all our powers to make that exact thing happen. What we aren't good at is looking at the big picture of where our variable fits in, and this can lead to problems. Consider for a moment:

- The fastest way to improve click-through rate for an ad is to make a sensational claim . . . even if it's false. Consequence: people lose trust in your brand.

- The easiest way to reduce the cost of a cosmetics package is to switch to an inferior package. Problem solved. Consequence: your brand suffers when the new package starts leaking, breaks under stress, or just feels cheap.

Optimizing for a single variable without taking other variables into account is usually a surefire way to completely screw things up in a complex system. In spite of how obvious this is, large organizations seem to specialize in turning their employees into single variable-focused machines, without any sense of the big picture. Luckily, these companies employ lots of highly paid MBAs who can figure out the big picture, right?

Unfortunately for large companies, MBAs are humans, too. They fall prey to the same misguided optimization problem that all other humans do. In large companies, it's quite common to see employees become obsessed with a variable called COGS. No, this has nothing to do with machines. COGS stands for Cost Of Goods Sold. It basically means the total cost of a product, excluding sales costs (marketing) and general overhead. COGS includes things such as cost of raw materials, packaging, and other similar expenses. It does not include the cost of things like research and development or salaries. Gross margin is the difference between the retail price and the COGS plus sales costs. Sales costs could be the cost of customer acquisition, including the margin you give to a retailer for selling your product.

Here it is in equation form:

$$[\text{Gross Margin}] = [\text{Retail Price}] - [\text{COGS}] - [\text{Sales Costs}]$$

Got that? Great.

Companies get obsessed with cutting COGS for a variety of reasons, but the most powerful is this: Wall Street gives strong preference to companies with high profit margins. Strong "preference" in this case translates to higher multiples (Price-vs.-Earnings ratio). In English, that means companies with higher profit margins have higher stock prices. In a world where much of executive compensation is tied to stock price, this means senior management has a strong incentive to keep profit margins high. And the easiest way to do that is to reduce costs.

The problem, however, is that when you start cutting costs, you may accidently cut out the very reason customers buy your products in the first place. For example, if a company creates a high-end product with exquisite but expensive packaging, swapping the packaging for something less expensive would reduce COGS, but simultaneously may leave customers with no reason to buy your product. This would, of course, reduce sales, to which a (wrong but common) response would be to cut COGS further. And the cycle continues.

Instead of opting for the simple but naïve approach of immediately cutting COGS in response to profit struggles, companies may be better served by investing in new sales channels or new product categories entirely where they aren't in a "race to the bottom" with competitors. For your purposes as a startup founder, just know that this dynamic is a crucial one within large companies. If a company is focused on COGS, every employee will be concerned and looking for ways to contribute a solution. This can be a tremendous opportunity for you, particularly if your technology or company helps the large organization reduce costs in the long term.

Conclusion and What's Next

As you've seen, the world of corporate has a culture and life of its own. Understanding the constraints and pressures on your corporate counterparts will help you better navigate the deal process as it progresses. Just as important, the fact that few startups work with large companies with an understanding for *their* needs will help set you up apart from competitors.

Next, we'll take a look at a phenomenon that is widely referred to, but whose true power is often underestimated—The Innovator's Dilemma.

CHAPTER 4

THE INNOVATOR'S DILEMMA IN ACTION

Before working in corporate, something that bothered me quite a bit was the fact that corporations have such large budgets and yet still have difficulty developing innovative new products. As startup founders, we are so used to cash being the limiting variable that we assume whoever has more of it is in a stronger position than we are. Yet this is not at all the case. This concept is so important that it is worth briefly examining before we move into the actual specifics of how to get deals done. Understanding why cash and company size aren't huge advantages (and can often be disadvantages) is key to fully realizing the value that you as a startup are actually providing to the large companies you are approaching. I'll go so far as to say that, in some instances, the startup shouldn't desperately be trying to sell to the large company; the large company should be selling the merits of working with them to the startup.

To better understand this, let's examine a case study of the market position of Airbnb versus traditional hotel brands.

Large hotel brands (such as Marriott or Hilton) have historically tried to build standardized experiences across their properties. For example, staying in a Residence Inn in New Jersey should be a very similar, if not identical, experience to staying at a Residence Inn in Florida. Over the past several decades, these companies have built processes to ensure that the guest experiences a consistent level of service.

In recent years, the rise of Airbnb has flipped this model on its head. Due to Airbnb's marketplace business model of connecting travelers to properties rented out by individuals, it is quite literally impossible for Airbnb to deliver a standard guest experience, even within the same city. Instead of viewing this as a negative, Airbnb has embraced this aspect of their business model and proudly proclaims that no two Airbnb properties are alike.

Travelers, too, seem to love this aspect of Airbnb, and now hotels are trying to figure out how to deal with this competitive threat. While hotels have the knowledge and resources to create unique experiences within each property, there are two main problems:

1. The infrastructure, processes, and mind-set of employees within hotel chains is all geared toward building consistency. While difficult and expensive to alter, culture (as all of these elements are) is ultimately fixable.

2. The marketing of hotel chains over dozens of years has emphasized consistency. Asking their customers to disbelieve past marketing is not only difficult, it can be damaging to the brand as well. This is far more difficult to effect.

At this point in the story, one may rightfully ask the question: When hotels saw the Airbnb threat incoming, why didn't they do anything about it? Why wouldn't they start their own competitor to Airbnb? After all, there's no intellectual property on Airbnb's business model—anyone can start a networking of properties to rent out to travelers. And no one had an existing consistent customer base of travelers like large hotel chains. It would seem trivial for a large hotel company to have squashed Airbnb in the early days.

This is where the Innovator's Dilemma enters the picture.

The Innovator's Dilemma

If you've been around the startup world at all over the past few years, whether in corporate, startup, venture capital, or some other part of the ecosystem, chances are you've heard the term "Innovator's Dilemma." This term was originated by Clayton Christensen, a legendary Harvard Business School professor who studied what causes great companies to fail. In his book *The Innovator's Dilemma: When New Technologies Cause Great Firms to Fail*, Christensen offers two major reasons for this phenomenon, specifically as it relates to new technologies and business models:

1. **Value to Innovation Is an S-Curve**

   Because innovation is an iterative process, when a new technology comes out, the value is often not all that great. Think about the first mobile phones—they were gigantic, not very portable, had horrible battery life, and cost a fortune. But as improvements are made, the technology becomes infinitely more useful to customers. As more and more improvements are made, however, there are diminishing returns to further innovation. Again, look at the mobile phone market in 2018: each new version of the iPhone is only marginally better than the previous model. For this reason, the middle of the S-Curve is where the most customer value is.

2. Incumbent-Sized Deals

Put simply, large companies have a much higher threshold to consider a project "worth it" than startups do. This, too, makes logical sense. Companies are often judged on their revenue and/or profit growth on a percentage basis. If a company is doing $1 million in revenue and a project has the potential to add $1 million to their revenue, it is obviously worth considering. However, if a company is doing $1 billion in revenue and the same $1 million opportunity comes along, the decision is not quite as simple. What is the opportunity cost to pursuing the $1 million project? What are the chances of success? Even if it succeeds, is there another, higher potential project we wouldn't be able to pursue because we've invested resources in this $1 million project?

The difficulty with this logical approach is that sometimes the $1 million project can turn into a billion-dollar project. It's just extremely difficult to tell in the early days. Also, as we discussed in the previous chapters, employees of large companies have an asymmetric risk profile—they are disproportionately rewarded for not messing up as opposed to unearthing new business opportunities. All these factors combine to stifle incumbents from pursuing new innovation opportunities.

"The Market Is Too Small"

As alluded to in the incumbent-sized-deal section above, large companies by definition have difficulty sorting between small opportunities and opportunities that may appear small at the moment but have potential to be massive. While employee incentives tell part of the story, company culture is also important. Some companies recognize the impossible task of sorting potential market size for nascent opportunities, and these companies figure out ways to incentivize or encourage employees (or at least certain departments) to explore new businesses.

In most large companies, however, employees need to defend an addressable market size in order to be given permission to work on an idea. And this addressable market size needs to be significant, which can be a Herculean task. As Table 4.1 shows, the world's largest companies make double or even triple digit *billions* of dollars per year in revenue. Creating a line of business that can affect that number is a monumental project.

Table 4.1: Large Company Annual Revenue	
Company Name	**Annual Revenue (2016)**
Ford	$151.8 Billion
Alphabet (Google parent company)	$89.5 Billion
Procter & Gamble	$65.3 Billion
Coca-Cola	$41.9 Billion

At the first startup I ever worked for, MomTrusted.com, we were putting a content partnership in place with Procter & Gamble. As we were working on the pitch, I was getting excited by the prospect of driving a few thousand dollars of incremental revenue per month to P&G and wanted to include that in our presentation. I'll never forget what Chaz Giles, then CEO of MomTrusted, told me: "For a company the size of P&G, a few thousand dollars doesn't even qualify as a rounding error."

While at first this statement is astounding (after all, a few thousand dollars can pay your rent for several months, even in a city like New York), it holds up under closer examination. Again, looking at the numbers in the table, even a project worth $1 million may not qualify as a rounding error. For this reason alone (and there are many others), large companies are extremely picky about which projects are worth pursuing. It isn't uncommon to hear incredibly innovative ideas floating around large companies, but it is extremely rare (in my experience, at least) to find large companies pursuing those opportunities internally.

Given the high revenue threshold for starting new projects within large companies, it's worth examining for a moment the process that startups use to determine whether or not to pursue new business opportunities. Typically, startups begin the process with customers. If a startup can find someone to pay for something, that is often what they will at least consider working on or developing and offering around. While this process works for startups, it probably isn't replicable by large companies, and it certainly isn't replicable at scale. It all comes back to the concept of opportunity. For many startups, even the ones working on game-changing technologies, revenue is at a premium. Any additional revenue is usually significant. Meanwhile, for large companies, this is clearly not the case, so incremental revenue projections need to be massive before companies will consider pursuing new projects.

Missing Major Trends

While the exact reasons are unclear, there are a couple of phenomena that are at least partially responsible for why large companies miss the major trends developing all around them. One of these is driven by the outer world, and the other is driven by human psychology.

The Pace of Innovation

Most of the time, the projects that large companies pass up on pursuing don't go anywhere. The vast, vast majority of ideas are too early, not innovative enough, or flat-out wrong. Yet, on the rarest of occasions a small idea can turn into a massive idea, and this is almost always missed by large companies, thanks to their policy of not pursuing small projects. This goes back to the S-Curve, which Clayton Christensen refers to often in *The Innovator's Dilemma*.

At the beginning of any new technology's life cycle, value and therefore revenue is going to be at a premium, simply because customers aren't benefiting that much (yet) from the new offering. But as the offering develops further, customers get additional value from it and are willing to pay more. The problem for large companies, especially in recent years, is that markets now move too fast for them to adopt a "wait-and-see" approach to new-product development. These days, it isn't uncommon for a new app to take less time to get from 100,000 downloads to a million downloads than it took to get from 0 to 100,000 downloads. In other words, thanks to modern marketing technologies (such as social media) and the continued "flattening of the world," it's easier than ever for products to grow exponentially.

Unfortunately for large companies, this increasingly frenzied pace of innovation means that it is becoming easier to miss major consumer trends and nearly impossible to catch up once they're behind (excluding major acquisitions, but that's a different discussion). Large companies are increasingly investing in new internal structures and organizations to help them stay on top of emerging trends, but these have proven difficult. Whether the internal structures are called "labs," "open innovation," "external innovation," or something else, they are still subject to the same dynamics as all large companies, namely that opportunities need the potential to be massive (whatever that means to the particular company) to be worth pursuing. But of course no one can tell the future or predict consumer trends with any accuracy, so the best ideas of the future often get completely overlooked.

Knowing that large companies face a systemic disadvantage by virtue of their size is one of the keys to understanding the under-the-radar power that savvy startups have over large companies.

Inattentional Blindness

There is a psychology experiment that, when I first heard about it, completely blew my mind and explained so much about the world. Those who have heard of the "invisible gorilla" know the experiment I am referring to; but for clarity, I will elaborate on it below.

In the late 1990s, Daniel Simons and Christopher Chabris designed a study in which they asked participants to watch a video of two groups of people (one wearing white shirts and the other wearing black shirts) passing a basketball around. In various versions of the experiment, participants are asked to count the number of passes made by one of the teams or to count the number of bounce passes versus aerial passes. At some point during the video, someone wearing a full gorilla suit walks through the scene. After watching the video, participants were asked if they noticed anything strange during the video. Shockingly (to me anyway), a full 50 percent of participants didn't notice *anything* amiss.

You might be thinking "so what?"—who cares if someone was able to spot a gorilla during a basketball-counting exercise? What does that have to do with anything? Well, in 2013, Trafton Drew, Melissa Vo, and Jeremy Wolfe conducted a follow-up experiment to test inattentional blindness among subject-matter experts, in this case radiologists. In this particular experiment, the experimenters inserted an image of a gorilla shaking its fist (in tribute to the original experiment) into a CT scan image. They then asked expert radiologists to look at the images for cancerous nodules, something they are well trained to do. Similar to the original experiment, the experimenters asked the radiologists if they noticed anything odd in the CT scans. This time, a whopping 83 percent of the participants missed the gorilla!

To my best knowledge, what these experiments are showing us is that when we are laser-focused on a particular task, whether that is counting passes, searching for cancerous nodules, or growing sales of our flagship product, our field of vision narrows to exclude anything outside our core goal. The world is an immensely complex place. Your brain needs some type of filter in order to focus and move toward your goal. This makes complete sense and seems to be the only way to make our way in the world without getting overwhelmed by the vast, vast complexity.

So, what does all this have to do with corporate innovation? Simply that, like everyone else, people who work for large companies are focused on the task in front of them. And a natural consequence of that focus is that they will miss trends that are, quite literally, staring them in the face. These blind spots are what lead to opportunity for startups and new market entrants. Once you understand the concept of inattentional blindness, it becomes less strange to see large companies miss major trend shifts. In fact, it becomes *more* shocking when you witness a company spot and react to a trend in a timely fashion.

The Startup's Hidden Power

If startups begin to understand the leverage they have with large companies, I'm convinced we will have a much healthier startup-corporate ecosystem. Likewise, large companies can solve their issue of being "too big" by creating better, low-risk systems for working with startups, especially those they may currently deem as being too small or not proven enough to pay attention to. As we'll discuss in much more detail in later chapters, startups and large companies have complementary natures that solve each other's problems.

In relation to the Innovator's Dilemma, startup-corporate relationships can serve numerous functions for large companies, which startups should know and take full advantage of.

Low-Risk/High-Reward Learning

One of the biggest advantages a large company has in relation to startups is monetary. Essentially, an amount of money that is significant for a startup is not necessarily significant for a large company. This dichotomy enables large companies to work with startups in an experimental, relatively low-risk way that still allows meaningful upside if an experiment works out.

To make this easier to conceptualize, assume that a corporate innovation group is tasked with exploring four different subject areas in order to come up with an innovative concept in each and has a $100,000 budget to either hire one employee or work with a few startups. While it's very difficult for one employee to come in and deliver value in four unrelated areas, working with four different startups is a lot more feasible.

But even more importantly, a pilot with a startup is not a recurring, ongoing type of thing. That means a $25,000 pilot is exactly that—$25,000. If it doesn't work out, there's no obligation to continue working together. And on the flip side, if the pilot is successful, the startup will of course be thrilled to expand the scope of the partnership.

In other words, the downside is completely protected and the upside is unlimited. That's the type of asymmetric advantage that all companies should strive for.

Easily Shift with Emerging Trends

If you've ever been around large companies, you know it takes a long time to get things moving. This isn't a matter of laziness or intellect—it mainly has to do with the complexity of coordinating a large group of people.

Contrast that with how quickly trends shift in the world today. It seems like there is a new cultural moment every few weeks, and those brands that can't keep up seem out of touch. But the brands that can stay on top of trends, especially on social media (Taco Bell and Dominos come to mind), create millions of dollars of earned media for themselves. The stakes are huge.

One solution to this trend adaptation is to work with startups at the forefront of the emerging trend. Again, this is a way to limit downside, exponentially increase speed, and access deep knowledge on complex subject areas.

An important point here to also consider is that it can be extremely difficult to distinguish between fad and trend. Working with startups in low-cost, low-risk ways is one way for a large company to avoid having to make this fad-vs.-trend distinction. If something is a fad, the company isn't locked in to a massive investment or a long-term deal. However, if it truly is a trend, there is a fairly simple path to doubling down with a more involved project.

Ears to the Ground

While large companies do have consumer insights, trends, and social listening resources (and sometimes even full departments), these groups have a lot of trouble spotting trends at the ground level before they reach "critical mass." There are a few reasons for this.

You may have noticed that most consumer-facing large companies (with a few exceptions) are in catch-up mode when it comes to consumer trends. One major reason this happens is that it is extremely difficult to distinguish between signal and noise without being in direct contact with the customer. This is a distinction between operations at startups vs. at large companies, which doesn't get enough attention: thanks to the customer-development focus popularized by books like *The Lean Startup* by Eric Ries, many different job functions within startups get regular contact with customers. Unfortunately, in large organizations, there are very few non-retail job functions that involve regular direct contact with customers. This is a major disadvantage, as having direct customer contact is the best way to have "ears to the ground" and understand what is bubbling beneath the surface of apparent trends (or fads).

It would be understandably difficult (though desirable) for a large company to build customer interactions into all their job functions. Luckily for large companies, working with startups is a great proxy for getting access to accurate customer information and data. This can take many forms. For some companies, particularly those further removed from the end customer (like manufacturers), there is enough value in simply hearing customer anecdotes to get a better sense for what the end user desires. In other instances, working with startups in a more formalized manner can provide the "front lines" data that the large company lacks. For digital startups, such as marketplaces, this can take the form of monthly or weekly reports, which the large company pays for, along with quarterly customer-facing sessions. Startups can get creative about the exact implementation; but simply knowing that direct customer interaction is a blind spot in the large-company capability stack is a valuable thing to know when crafting win-win deals.

Dave Knox, author of Predicting the Turn, co-founder of The Brandery startup accelerator in Cincinnati and CMO of Rockfish (acquired by WPP), believes interacting with startups holds incredible value for large companies:

Startups are, in many ways, the canary in the coal mine for big companies today. They can be the warning system for changes that are taking place in the marketplace. It's a really interesting thing for a large company to be able to engage with

(continued on next page)

(continued from previous page)

a startup and see how they are impacting and changing the industry, before it has even played out. It's hugely valuable. You could almost argue that startups are the new R&D for large companies.

To read more of Dave's thoughts on the startup-corporate ecosystem, please find his full interview in the Appendix.

Perception Advantage

Last but certainly not least is the perception advantage that working with startups can lend to large companies. There are advantages to this that have far-reaching, often surprising effects.

The easiest perception advantage to point to is share price. While the stock market is incredibly complicated on some levels, on other levels it is childishly simplistic. This is one of those simplistic cases: share prices for companies that are perceived as innovative do better than shares of companies perceived as dinosaurs. Crazy, I know. And executives are often compensated on share-price performance. It doesn't take a genius to connect the dots and realize that there is a strong incentive for large companies to have themselves perceived as innovative by creating programs that make it easier for them to work with startups. And as a side note, executives love showing investors case studies that show innovative new partnerships and programs, even if those programs didn't necessarily contribute a whole lot to the bottom line. These case studies allow executives to craft a favorable narrative. This is extremely valuable.

Another perception advantage comes in recruiting. Companies spend billions of dollars collectively on recruiting new employees to work with them. Again, companies that have a perception of being "on the cutting edge" and innovative have a much easier time of recruiting than companies that are perceived as "out of touch." Who would want to go work at a stodgy old company, when you can choose a company that is "changing the world"?

Finally, working with innovative startups is a great way to keep existing employees excited about their work. While not completely new, the influx of "startup media" celebrating innovation (outlets like *Fast Company*, *Harvard Business Review*, *Business Insider*, *Forbes*, and others are good examples) does put a bit of pressure on employees to work on innovative projects. If a company feels out of step, which is an especially big risk at older large companies, the organization risks losing its top talent to better perceived businesses. Working with outside startups to accomplish corporate goals goes a long way toward satisfying top-tier employees' longing for innovative work, leading to lower employee turnover and higher employee satisfaction.

All these perceived advantages add up to create a "rich get richer" scenario, where a perceived advantage of being "startup-friendly" leads more startups to reach out to certain large companies who, by virtue of a stronger lead funnel, have better, more publicized results when working with startups, which again leads more startups to reach out to them, and so on and so forth. This virtuous cycle is the holy grail for corporate innovation groups, one that startup founders should keep in mind when crafting the narrative for their deals with large companies.

What's Coming Next

Now that you have a strong handle on the inner workings of large companies, the decision-making process, and the reasons why innovation within large companies is so difficult, we'll get into more detail of how exactly to get an enterprise deal done. In the next chapter, you'll find a step-by-step guide for initiating and closing an enterprise deal. Then we'll get into major mistakes that startups make when trying to partner with or sell to large companies. Finally, we'll examine the biggest deal type of all: taking an investment from a large company.

Buckle up.

2

WORKING WITH CORPORATE INNOVATORS TO DRIVE GROWTH FOR YOUR STARTUP

CHAPTER 5

HOW TO
GET A DEAL DONE
The Complete Guide

Now that you have a strong understanding of how large companies work internally, we'll discuss the topic that you (hopefully) bought this book to learn about: how to actually get deals done from start to finish.

How Startup-Corporate Deals Work: A Primer and a Word of Warning

Before diving into the step-by-step process of getting a deal started and closed, I want to quickly set expectations (side note: this is also a good thing to do when starting sales conversations).

Closing deals with large companies takes time. Often lots of time. If your strategy involves corporate deals, I strongly advise making sure you have enough funding and runway to handle a sales process that can take twelve months (and sometimes longer) until you actually start getting paid. This cannot be overemphasized. Startups are all about speed, but unfortunately it is next to impossible to speed up large companies (though it does happen occasionally). Trust me: if you understand that these deals will take twelve months and plan for it, you will be a lot less stressed about each individual interaction in the sales process.

Something I've seen almost universally among inexperienced founders is the (naïve) belief that they'll be able to close a six- or seven-figure deal in a single meeting. If you've been around inexperienced founders (or perhaps you've been one yourself; I certainly have been), you've probably heard something along the lines of "once I'm in the room and am able to give our pitch with the decision-maker, there's no way we're walking out of there without a deal." If you've been doing sales or business development for longer than six months and/or you've spent any amount of time working with large companies, you know it just doesn't work like that. Even the most no-brainer deal requires a myriad of steps: buy-in from multiple stakeholders, budgeting conversations, approval from the legal department, discussions about the rollout plan, and more.

More than anything else, getting a deal done with a large company is about risk mitigation.

In 2017, I was attending a marketing conference where the Marketing Analytics Director for one of the oldest, largest, and most prestigious media companies in the world was speaking. During the question-and-answer session, one of the attendees asked which new media and social platforms the media company was taking advantage of to reach new audiences. As the analytics director launched into his answer, one thing he said struck me as incredible: "Obviously, we're on Snapchat." As one of the biggest social platforms in the world, it didn't strike me as odd that this company was on Snapchat. However, I was stunned at how much of a shift Snapchat had made in their brand perception in such a short period of time. As recently as 2014, most prestigious media brands would have scoffed at the idea of using an ephemeral platform like Snapchat to reach consumers. Yet not even three years later, using Snapchat for content distribution was so obvious that "of course" was used as a qualifier to describe it.

While just an anecdote, the prestigious-media-brand story highlights a major opportunity and task for startups in their growth journeys. In 2014, working with a company like Snapchat was risky, at least from a perception standpoint if not also in reality. There weren't enough proof points of well-known brands using Snapchat effectively to mitigate the risk of being embarrassed if (or when) something didn't quite work as expected. Yet just three years later, there was so much social proof that *not* being on Snapchat as a major media company would have been more controversial than being on it.

The point here is that this highlights your task as a founder or salesperson trying to work with large corporations: make working with your startup something that your corporate counterpart would get in trouble for *not* doing.

The Seven Stages of Startup-Corporate Deals . . . and Dating

Closing a startup-corporate deal is a lot like dating. Seems like a stretch? Not as much as you might think. Stick with me here. Here are the typical steps in a startup-corporate deal, along with their dating counterparts:

1. Getting an Introductory Meeting (Asking Someone Out)
2. Introductory Meeting (First Date)
3. Follow-up Meetings (Dates 2–N)
4. Pilot Project (First Night Together)
5. Discussions on How to Scale Up (Considering Getting Married)
6. Scale Up & Signing a Contract (Getting Engaged)
7. Implementation (Marriage)

As I said, more similar than it might initially appear.

Depending on what your company is offering and who you're offering it to, the steps listed above can take varying amounts of time. Similarly, the stages can take different amounts of time for different companies. Some business models can get to pilot projects in a matter of weeks, but then the pilot itself will take twelve months. Others can take a year or more to get to a pilot but then can validate their concept through the pilot in a couple of weeks. The steps outlined above are generally true for any startup-corporate deal and can be used as a guideline for understanding how far along you are in the process and how far you have to go. We'll examine each of these steps in detail throughout this chapter; but for now, suffice it to say that every deal you work on with a large corporation will follow some variation of the steps outlined above.

Moving Forward: Risk Mitigation

As we've outlined throughout the book so far, large companies and the individuals who work for them usually think in terms of risk mitigation. While this happens for a variety of reasons and may or may not be explicitly recognized by the individuals who work within the large companies, risk mitigation is what drives deals forward. When examining the deal phases listed above, it is therefore essential that you think about reducing the risk at each step in the process.

More concretely, each stage in the process is riskier than the previous one. For example, taking an introductory meeting with you isn't risky at all. If the introductory meeting takes one hour, at most, the corporate employee is losing an hour of their time. However, a pilot project will cost the corporate employee money, time, and reputation and will therefore require a higher burden of proof to move forward. Reputation is the biggest cost of all: by championing a project with your company, your corporate counterpart is now fully invested in the success of the project. If it fails, not only is the budget allocated to the project wasted, but the project is also a stain on the employee's track record. This can be difficult to recover from. Therefore, when trying to move deals forward, it is essential to think about how to mitigate risk along the way. We'll examine this in more detail in later sections.

Internal Champions and Decision-Makers: A Primer

While much of this chapter focuses on the decision-maker, which is usually the individual with budget authority, there is another type of person that's worth searching for: the internal champion. The champion is going to be crucial in giving your deal the momentum to move forward—especially when roadblocks arise, as they inevitably will. While the champion and the decision-maker can be the same individual (and in ideal situations, they are), this is not a requirement and doesn't happen very often. The champion should be someone of influence who has enough clout within the organization to make recommendations.

Sebastian Metti, founder of Resolute Innovation, walked us through his company's process in successfully closing deals:

Big successes take a committed team on the startup side and corporate side. Most importantly, there should be several champions ideally on the corporate side. For Resolute, we experienced our biggest successes when we were able to identify, collaborate, and grow with champions spanning key decision groups. Because a startup product is never complete, it's rarely fully aligned with the specific needs of the buyer. Collaborating with identified champions meant we were actively listening to their needs, soliciting feedback, and applying advice on how to better align the product, whether that meant building new features, adding new data, or improving the user experience. As we got the feedback from our champions, we built a product that was more aligned with their needs and those of future customers. This entire sales journey also demonstrated our commitment to customer success, which is important to large corporate partners who are taking a risk by giving time and money to a startup. In the end, we were able to score a massive deal with the company after over a year of searching the company for champions, collaborating with them on product-customer alignment, and building value through a better product. It's a big success because we built a better product and won a high-revenue account.

To learn more about Resolute Innovation and their groundbreaking artificial intelligence for intellectual property platform, please visit: www.resoluteinnovation.com.

Finding an ideal corporate champion is ultimately a matter of quality versus quantity. It's much better to have one corporate champion who is obsessed with your product than to have ten individuals within the company who are vaguely interested in the product but not so much in love with it that they would stake their reputation on pushing for its adoption. And ultimately, what you need is obsession to get through the steps that might be involved in taking a deal from start to finish.

Deal Pipeline

The long time lines involved in these startup-corporate deals are often worrying to founders. This is quite understandable. After all, investing twelve months or longer trying to close a deal that ultimately doesn't go through could be devastating, not just emotionally but also to your company's morale. How does a smart founder or sales leader go about solving this problem?

The solution to this problem is to build a portfolio of deals that you pursue simultaneously. Each of these deals will progress at different rates and may even be initiated at different times, so it's normal to have some deals in the pilot stage while others are still in the introductory-meeting phase.

A portfolio approach is also how you avoid the devastated feeling that losing a major deal can bring. Obviously, investing months or even a year into a deal only to see it fall apart is a horrible feeling for anyone. But that feeling is a lot easier to swallow when you have twenty other deals in the pipeline to work on. Building this "plenty of fish in the sea" mentality is essential for a sales organization to be sustainable. Putting too much hope into any one deal is a risky proposition, no matter how much sense that deal may seem to make on the surface. Humans, for some reason that's above my pay grade, are extremely driven by narrative and momentum. When a company is closing deals left and right, it's almost a self-fulfilling prophecy that more deals will continue to close, even if the deals have nothing to do with each other directly. And yet the opposite is true as well: when a big deal falls apart, the negativity can "infect" the rest of the deals the company is working on. For this reason, I'm a firm believer in the portfolio approach, along with not putting too much stock into any one deal. The best sales leaders I've ever worked for followed this approach as well.

In addition to the internal-momentum argument, pursuing multiple deals can also be one of the few ways to entice large companies to make decisions more quickly, especially if you're speaking with multiple companies who compete with each other. As we'll discuss in more detail later, large companies often care about exclusivity, particularly within their industry, for potentially disruptive new technologies. This focus on exclusivity means that if you're speaking with two companies in the same sector, you can mention that there's another player (even if you don't name the company) and increase the urgency on both sides.

Finally, making use of a portfolio of deals helps add predictability and the ability to forecast to your sales pipeline. Each stage in the process can be assigned a probability of closing, along with a potential deal dollar value. These two numbers, combined with the stage of each deal, gives you an "expected value," which you can use to quantify your pipeline. Of course, the numbers you use to estimate the probability of closing at each stage will be based on an educated guess in the early days of your company; but as time goes on, you'll have historical data to calculate the actual percentages. Here's an example to make this easier to understand:

Deal 1

Stage: Pilot (50 percent chance of closing)

Potential Value: $10,000 per year

Expected Value: $5,000

Deal 2

Stage: Introductory Meeting (10 percent chance of closing)

Potential Value: $50,000 per year

Expected Value: $5,000

Deal 3

Stage: Scale Up Conversation, post-pilot (75 percent chance of closing)

Potential Value: $20,000 per year

Expected Value: $15,000

As you can see, the total expected value of the simplified pipeline above is $25,000. This value is derived by weighing the total deal value with the percentage chance of closing, based on the stage the deal is currently at in the process. This now allows you to quantitatively determine if your sales pipeline is growing or shrinking, week to week and quarter to quarter. Many customer relationship management (CRM) systems will do this calculation for you automatically.

Long story short: use a portfolio approach if enterprise sales are part of your growth strategy.

The Payoff

After all the caveats given in this chapter, you may be wondering if you should reconsider working with or selling to large companies. Since I've made the process sound like a nightmare, this is understandable. However, working with large companies isn't all bad news; in fact, depending on your company, it's very much worth the time investment involved.

Done correctly, the sheer size of corporate deals can make the time, pain, and effort more than worth it. Six-figure deals are definitely in the realm of possibility when working with large companies. In contrast, imagine how many small businesses you would need to sell a $500 product to in order to hit $100,000 in revenue. If you can pull in just ten deals of $100,000+ with large companies, you have a business turning over more than a million dollars per year. And that's with just ten customers.

Besides revenue, there are other reasons to go through the effort of working with large companies. One major reason is market validation. Even if your largest market segment is comprised of small businesses, having well-known brands as customers gives you the validation you need for your small-business customers to trust you. Having a well-known, trusted brand listed on your website as a customer can do more for driving new sales than ten salespeople. Another, often-overlooked benefit to working with large companies is ease of recruiting. Similar to potential customers and investors, potential employees are looking to your customer base for validation that your startup has a sustainable idea that has lasting power. In other words, they don't want to start working for a company that will be out of business in six months. Having brand-name customers is a great way to show potential employees that there are smart people out there who have validated that your company is doing important work.

Deal Stages and How to Navigate Them

As we discussed earlier in this chapter, the process for closing a deal with a large company usually takes the following stages, now presented in a condensed, five-step format:

1. Getting an Introductory Meeting
2. Introductory Meeting
3. Follow-Up Meetings
4. Pilot Projects
5. Scale Up & Implementation

We'll now go through each of these stages in detail as well as the process for moving things forward to the next stage.

Getting an Introductory Meeting

To get an introductory meeting that has the potential to lead to a deal, you first need to figure out who to meet with. The ideal person to meet with is someone who has decision-making authority. However, while ideal, this isn't always possible, so navigating the corporate hierarchy to meet with someone who has access to a decision-maker is a great second option. Keep in mind that these introductory meetings aren't a "one and done" type of situation. It may take three, five, or even ten introductory meetings to get to the right person. Finding the decision-maker isn't simple: no one has the words "decision-maker" on their LinkedIn profile or stamped on their forehead. The best way to think about finding the right person is to think of the process as a scavenger hunt. Each meeting you have helps you build a more accurate map of that particular company's hierarchy and corporate landscape. Every meeting and interaction will yield further clues that get you closer to the person or group you need to be meeting with. As long as you eventually get to the right people, all this effort and searching is worth it.

Innovation Teams

For better or worse, most Fortune 500 companies have innovation groups. These groups are sometimes organized by vertical or business unit (i.e., process innovation group, or product innovation group), but can also be more general and service the entire organization. Among startup founders and those selling to large companies, there are mixed feelings on innovation groups. On one hand, innovation groups often lack budgets and authority to do a large deal. There is also a strong incentive to meet with as many companies as possible—an unfortunate quantity-over-quality approach. On the other hand, innovation groups tend to be very well connected within large companies and often play the role of internal connector.

It's difficult to understand this from the outside; but, as we've discussed earlier, individual departments within large companies act more as islands than intertwined teammates. Some of this is caused by the curse of specialization; but, more often, it's just that different departments don't interact very much in their day-to-day roles. However, innovation often takes place at the intersection of fields or subjects, so innovation projects usually involve multiple departments that don't know each other very well. For this reason, innovation departments often act as a bridge or connector for projects at the intersections of multiple subjects.

Starting your search for an internal decision-maker with the innovation group is not a bad strategy if you understand that they are most likely not going to be able to do a deal in isolation. Innovation groups are usually open to discussions (it's their job, after all) and can be really helpful if you can show that you're working on something interesting. In particular, innovation-group employees are helpful in giving you a landscape of the entire company, the different departments, who is responsible for what functions, and, most importantly, what each group is ultimately judged on. All of this information is extremely hard to get from the outside and is exactly what makes innovation teams a great place to start building your map for the corporate structure of your target company.

Learning Conversations

Remember how we discussed risk mitigation as the key to getting corporate deals done? Well, sometimes a new label is all you need to reduce the risk of a sales conversation. Said more clearly, asking someone for a "sales meeting" is a great way to get shut down. The only way this request is going to work is if the target already explicitly knows that they are looking for a solution to their problem, has budgeted for it, *and* has a strong belief that your solution is going to solve their problem. That's a tall order.

However, a tactic that often works is to have a learning conversation with the target group. Getting one of these conversations isn't all that difficult, especially if you go through an innovation group. For example, if you are meeting with a corporate innovation group and they mention that you'll need to have buy-in from the "Process Engineering Department," a request that is fairly likely to get a "Yes" is asking your counterpart if they might be able to set up a conversation with someone from the Process Engineering Department so that you might be able to learn as you develop your product and future feature road map. This is a really simple, easy, and, most importantly, risk-free ask of your corporate counterpart. Even better, you're actually making your corporate innovation counterpart look great within their company and show their usefulness by giving *them* the opportunity to set up a meeting. That's a win-win way to get your foot in the door.

Titles and Decision-Makers

When I first started selling to large companies, I would get very impressed by people with "Vice President" in their title. That title must mean they are extremely powerful, right? Second in command!

Little did I know that large companies give out "VP" titles like people giving away candy on Halloween. In some companies, VPs don't even have the ability to make their own budget decisions. Other companies have multiple tiers of VPs: Associate Vice President (AVP), Senior Vice President (SVP), Executive Vice President (EVP), etc., etc.

Yet in other companies, VPs DO actually have budget authority and can make decisions. It's just really difficult to tell from the outside. Assuming you're talking to the decision-maker because they have "Vice President" in their title is a common but avoidable error.

My suggestion would be to start at the VP or Director level if possible and work your way from there, understanding that you may have to have several introductory meetings before getting the attention of the decision-maker.

LinkedIn and Email Guessing

Confession: I don't understand why LinkedIn is such a hated tool. Yes, their user experience and design leaves much to be desired. Yes, there are a lot of spammers on the site. Yes, there are way too many people who want to "connect" and be "thought leaders." But that doesn't take away from one major benefit of LinkedIn: it's the easiest way to find people in key roles within the companies you are trying to target.

Once you know who you're trying to reach, the next step is finding your target's email. There are plenty of services you can use to get access to verified emails, but simple guesswork will often suffice. Most companies use a few possible formats for their emails:

firstname.lastname@company.com

firstinitiallastname@company.com

lastname_firstname@company.com

firstname_lastname@company.com

If you're sending out more than fifty or so outbound sales emails per month, it's probably worth your time to pay for a service to verify the emails for you.

Sending a Cold Email

The art of sending a cold email is an elusive one. A cold emailer has a tall task in front of them. They need to make their subject line, email, and themselves come across as useful, interesting, and vaguely mysterious. At the same time, the email can't come across as sleazy, salesy, or creepy. And it also can't be too long.

While specifics for cold emails depend on your industry and target customer profile, there is a general structure that seems to work best:

Dear _____,

Hope this email finds you doing well!

I'm reaching out after coming across your LinkedIn profile while researching [INSERT COMPANY HERE]. We have some professional contacts in common (including Jane Doe, who I just had lunch with last month). Basically, I really wanted to connect given your experience building the [COMPANY NAME] Consumer Experience Innovation group.

For context, our company creates in-store widgets that increase shopper time in store by 42% and increase average basket size by 26%. We're doing this with companies like [NAME BRAND CUSTOMER 1] and [NAME BRAND CUSTOMER 2]. The best part about working with us is [INSERT ROI or price metric here].

At your convenience, I'd love to share more about our projects and business model to see if there's an opportunity for us to partner.

Hope to hear from you soon!

Best Regards,

Neil

There are a few things I'd like to point out about the cold email example above:

- Noting any mutual contacts early on in the email will increase the likelihood that the recipient will read on.
- Showing that you've done your research (such as noting their role) early on will increase the likelihood that the recipient will read on.
- Including numbers, like X% improvement of metrics that you know your target customer cares about, increases the likelihood that they will respond. Same with including name brands.

A Quick Note on Outbound Email Services

There are services out there that will handle the cold emailing work for you. While useful, in the early stages I suggest doing this work yourself. Seeing what gets responses and what doesn't is the best way to figure out what's resonating with your target customer. Once you have this figured out, working with an outbound email service makes more sense.

Conclusion: The Numbers Game

As unsophisticated as it sounds, getting introductory meetings is often a numbers game. A poorly constructed cold email may have a 1 percent chance of response. A well-constructed one still might only have a 10 percent chance. Enterprise employees get tons of emails (both internal and external) every day, and even great cold emails can fall through the cracks. On top of that, you might just catch someone on a bad day and not get a response. And it's usually not your fault.

For this reason, *outbound volume* is extremely important for generating enough introductory meetings to service your lead funnel. Of course, you want to do ample research to construct the best possible cold email, but you don't want to do so much research that you only have time to send two emails per day. The key is finding a balance.

Setting Up and Running an Introductory Meeting

It's not at all uncommon to enjoy a feeling of victory after getting a response saying that your corporate prospect would like to meet with you. While understandable, please try to avoid this feeling if at all possible. It's important to celebrate small wins, no doubt, but getting an introductory meeting is only 5 percent of the battle (and maybe less).

Now we're going to discuss what to do once you have an introductory meeting scheduled and how to run the meeting like a pro to ensure that you can progress the deal.

Preparing for the Meeting

As Sun Tzu once (supposedly) said: "Every battle is won before it is fought." In that same vein, the success (or failure) of your corporate interactions is going to be driven in large part by your preparation work.

First and foremost, you need to understand what your prospect company actually does. Not just on the surface, but at a deeper level: which sectors they are in, how many employees they have, which countries they operate in, any major news or acquisitions, and anything else that might be top of mind for the individuals you are meeting with. This can usually be found by looking at the company's Wikipedia page and corporate website. This is not to be confused with their brand website, which is usually for customer-facing information, as opposed to investor- or corporate-related information.

You should also—and this may be obvious, but it needs to be said—make sure you know the name of the company you're speaking with. There were several introductory meetings I took while at Estée Lauder where the person pitching us confused us with L'Oréal, or even worse, thought we were owned by L'Oréal. Nothing could be further from the truth—and in fact, ELC views L'Oréal as their main competitor. Needless to say, this did not get things off to a great start.

A word of caution about company news: know enough of the latest company news to show that you've done your homework, but don't spend a large part of the pitch focused on it, and also don't assume that your corporate counterpart even cares. A large organization with 50,000 employees (for example) has divisions of the company that never come in contact with each other. While at the highest level they might be affected by a big acquisition or major partnership, in their day-to-day there may be no effect whatsoever. The two major goals of being up to speed on your target company's news are to know if there's anything directly affecting the group you're meeting with, and to show that you've done your homework.

A related point is to know the people you're meeting with. LinkedIn and Google are great tools for this. It's fairly common for two to five people to be added to the meeting from the corporate side. You'll be able to see their names and emails in the event invite; so before the meeting, make sure you look them up to get a sense for their backgrounds. Things will go much better for you if you do.

Before diving into specifics for the cadence and flow of an introductory meeting, let's take a quick second to talk about pitch decks. Having a sales deck is a necessary evil and can even be a useful tool if done right. The key is to make your deck complement what you are saying verbally instead of the (common) mistake of filling your slides with text. This just leads to people reading instead of listening and responding to you, which is the only way to build a dialogue and trust.

Sometimes companies will ask you to send along a deck or one-pager ahead of taking an introductory meeting. In these instances, you're going to want to have a deck that can be read on its own and doesn't need someone explaining it. This will be different than your presentation sales deck and should have enough information to whet their appetite to learn more but not so much that they get lost in the weeds.

An introductory sales meeting (like most meetings) typically begins with pleasantries. A great way to "break the tension" and get the other side talking is to ask them to go around and give a brief introduction of their name and role. Make sure you really understand who is in the room. Ask questions! People love talking about themselves, so these questions are definitely not going to be viewed as intrusive or out of place. You also will need to figure out (in a broad sense) what each person in the room cares about, what they're being judged on, and how you can possibly help.

Before you even dive into your deck, give a succinct overview of what your company does. Think of this as your "elevator pitch," which grounds everyone into the same frame of reference before getting into the nitty-gritty details of your offering. In rare instances, the group you're meeting with may latch on to something in your initial overview and get into questions right away. Don't be scared—this is a great thing; it shows that they are genuinely interested in working together. If the conversation gets going before you present the deck, then forget about the deck! You can always share that with them later. The whole point of the meeting was to get a better sense of where your solution could fit and to help solve their problems. I've seen founders push to present the deck at all costs, but this doesn't do anything to help their cause. Sometimes you just need to go with the flow.

Once you get past introductory pleasantries, overview, and deck presentation, it's time to dig deeper to get some sense for the need you're solving and why they would care. Sometimes this is prompted by your corporate counterparts, but other times you'll have to search and probe with questions of your own. When presenting the offering, the key is to keep things broad enough so corporate can project their own needs and desires onto it, but specific enough that there's actually something to grasp.

Follow-up Meetings

Before diving into this section, I'd like to point one thing out: sometimes, you'll be able to get a pilot project or contract straight from an introductory meeting. This is extremely rare, especially with large companies. The reason for this is that even if your introductory meeting was with the decision-maker, the decision-maker will rarely be the person with enough "on-the-ground" knowledge to discuss implementation. So be prepared for follow-up meetings.

Types of Follow-up Meetings

There are a few different types of follow-up meetings, listed in order of usefulness to the closing process:

1. Implementation Specifics
2. New Stakeholders
3. Update/Checking-in Meetings

Implementation Specifics Meeting

If you're given a meeting to talk implementation specifics, that's great news. It means the company is pretty sure that they want to work with you. Obviously, nothing is signed at this point, so don't make any assumptions; but talking implementation specifics is not something corporate innovation folks do with every company they meet. If you're at this stage of the process, you need to be careful to not scare the large company away. Things that can scare large companies include long contracts, large up-front payments, and huge technological infrastructure changes. But as long as you play your cards right, if you're in this type of meeting you should at least be able to get a pilot project set up.

New Stakeholders

As we've discussed, decision-making in large organizations is usually more of a matrix than a direct line. To that end, even after a great meeting with the decision-maker, there is a strong possibility that she will have to include other stakeholders, such as other department heads, before any kind of deal (even a pilot) can move forward.

For example, with a cosmetics company, if you're selling a technology that enhances packaging, you may think you only need the approval of the packaging department. This is not true. Because package and product interact (aka touch each other), the group responsible for product will also need to be involved, or at least kept in the loop. Remember, bringing additional stake-holders into the fold isn't done simply for practical reasons; it also serves a CYA (cover your ass) function: if multiple stake-holders are involved, any possible blame for a failed project can be spread out over more people. This dynamic cannot be stressed enough—it is truly at the root of many corporate behaviors.

When new stakeholders are brought into the fold, keep in mind that they are starting with a clean slate. And just like with any introductory meeting, do your best to understand what they care about and what they are being judged on. For example, if the new stakeholder's role is to ensure a consistent consumer experience for their customers, don't spend a ton of time touting the opportunities to create new revenue. That simply doesn't affect them. Instead, share how your product integrates seam-lessly with the company's existing platform and doesn't require any major user experience changes.

Chaz Giles, formerly of Citi Ventures, P&G, and MomTrusted. com and currently Global Head of External Innovation at The Estée Lauder Companies, advised startups to spend more time listening than speaking once they have a foot in the door:

I'm still surprised at how many founders keep conversations in sales mode, instead of progressing them to strategic partner mode. Obviously, at the beginning you're selling—you need to get in the door. But once you have a receptive conversation, the ratio of speaking to listening needs to change dramatically. The goal at that point is about listening to that organization and understanding the itches, the pain points—and hooking your solution to those itches and pain points.

(continued on next page)

(continued from previous page)

In startups, the KPIs (Key Performance Indicators) and goals are usually somewhat straightforward. When dealing with large organizations, these things are not at all obvious. There can be nuances that affect what someone gets their bonus for. For example, if I'm given a bonus for streamlining procurement and you're a startup selling in and complicating things, that means that you are literally moving my key metric in the wrong direction—even if the startup is very, very valuable.

This can show up in a variety of other ways, too. For example, contract structure: a company may be trying to reduce their recurring costs. So by structuring your contract with a lower recurring cost but a higher success fee, you may be increasing the overall cost of the deal, but the *individual* you are dealing with doesn't care about overall cost: they only care about recurring cost. But you would only know that by listening and understanding what people are measured on and rewarded for.

To read Chaz's complete interview, please visit the Appendix.

Update/Check-in Meetings

This is the most common and nebulous type of follow-up meeting and could mean all sorts of things. On one hand, getting a second meeting probably means that you're not out of the game yet. But on the other hand, it's totally possible (perhaps even likely) to get a second meeting with your corporate counterpart having no real intention to move things forward. This dynamic is similar to (most) venture capitalists. It's rare for a VC to give you an outright "no" when you try to raise money. Instead, they may tell you to come back when you hit a certain revenue number or close an enterprise customer. But really, there is no intention to do a deal.

Why this two-faced dynamic? There is simply no advantage for a VC (or a corporate innovator) to give you an outright "no." No one can predict the future: six months from now, your startup may be the hottest company in the industry and the large company doesn't want to alienate you precisely because that is a possibility.

For this reason, update and check-in meetings are usually not anything to get too excited about. Yet it is important that you do them regularly. This is known as "lead nurturing," and it's part of the dance of closing an enterprise deal. Why is this necessary? Corporate needs are always changing. Something they might not have needed four months ago might be a top priority today. While it's sometimes possible to figure out how the need set is changing from the outside, it is rare and usually much more effective to learn about changing needs directly from the company you are trying to sell to.

A usually foolproof way to get check-in meetings scheduled is to mention new features you've developed or, even better, new customers you are working with—to your corporate counterpart. It is very difficult for someone in corporate to say no to an email like that.

This update/check-in dance may last weeks. It may last months. And in some instances, it may take years. Play the long game and keep it going. And have a large-enough pipeline that you can survive to play the long game.

Pilot Projects

More often than not, large companies will require a pilot project before you do a full implementation. This is true, no matter how simple you make the process, how easy to implement your product is, or how risk-free your proposal is. Large companies almost always want to test you out before committing to anything.

The most frustrating thing about all this is that it makes complete sense. Startups are almost always playing offense: startups have very little market share, almost no brand, and not much name recognition. Large companies, on the other hand, are playing defense. They have a lot to lose if something doesn't go well or leads to bad press. A negative press article can reduce their publicly traded market cap by literally billions of dollars overnight. For this reason, large companies need to be sure that you can follow through on what you promise before they give you large projects.

The most common way for large companies to take your product out for a test drive is to implement a pilot project. This is usually a paid project of limited scope that allows the company to collect data on customer feedback, experience, revenue, and more.

Elements of a Well-Structured Pilot Project

There are several elements involved in designing a well-structured pilot project.

Pre-defined Goals

A middle-school teacher of mine once said, "You can't get anywhere unless you know where you're going." Without pre-defining what a successful pilot project looks like, it'll be extremely difficult to meet or exceed expectations, something that will need to happen in order to expand the contract from a pilot to a full-scale implementation. Some things you must absolutely be cognizant of when setting goals for the pilot:

- **Achievable Goals:** First and foremost, make sure the goals you set are achievable in the time frame and scope defined for the pilot. There's nothing worse than setting a goal you aren't capable of achieving. That's like shooting yourself in the foot and then trying to win a race.

- **Meaningful Goals:** Another common error is setting goals that aren't indicative of what you bring to the table. Remember, your corporate counterpart is using the results of the pilot to extrapolate the value your startup is going to provide at scale. Setting a goal that is too conservative isn't going to show you in your best light.

- **Quantifiable Goals:** While not everything can be measured, when defining the goals of your pilot, make sure you pick metrics that are easily quantifiable. It does you no good in closing the deal if you focus on metrics which that be potentially valuable but can't be quantified.

Responsibility for Management

It may seem attractive at first, but sharing responsibility for the pilot with your corporate counterparts is a dangerous game. Instead, lines of responsibility should be clearly defined going in. For example, you may determine that customer-facing elements are managed by the corporate partner, while product-related issues are managed by you. Or you may say that corporate is responsible for marketing and consumer-facing language, while you handle the fulfillment process. No matter how you decide to divide the responsibility, make sure that you actually do divide it.

Regular Check-ins

Communication is essential to a successful pilot. Like any new launch, it's rare to get things right the first time. Instead, a successful pilot will result from setting a good foundation and then iterating along the way. Communication is key to determining and implementing the right pivots. Make sure you schedule regular check-ins with your corporate counterpart. The exact intervals will be determined by the nature of your product and partnership.

Pilot Project Pitfalls to Avoid

When structuring pilot projects, there are a few pitfalls to avoid.

Pricing

I am a strong advocate for paid pilot projects. Why? Simple: skin in the game. Without skin in the game, your corporate partner has no reason to take the pilot seriously. This means that not only will your pilot not lead to an actual contract, but it won't even be given the attention it deserves. In contrast, if your counterpart is spending money from their budget for the project, you can bet they will be keeping a close eye on the results and give you the support you need for it to go well. Their reputation is just as much at stake as yours.

All too often, startups are willing to discount their pilots to free and then wonder why they struggle to convert pilots to contracts. We've been taught badly to think that price is the limiting reason why our meetings aren't converting to pilots. In most cases, however, this is simply not true.

The exact price you charge is less important, but make sure it's enough that a corporate budget will feel it as an item. You don't want to charge $200 for a pilot project. Also make sure that it is representative of your actual pricing. It makes no sense to test a price of $2,000/month if your true price is $20,000/month.

Timing

The length of your pilot should be determined by the user or customer cycle of your product or service. Does it take three months for a customer to go through the full cycle of the product? Six months? A year? The pilot length should be determined by your product life cycle, not some arbitrary length of time.

Scale-up and Implementation

Pilot projects are wonderful, but remember that pilot projects are simply one more step on the way to a full-scale contract. The real goal is to get beyond the pilot. To that end, planning for the scale-up and full-scale implementation is essential.

Successfully scaling up is no small task. With Fortune 500 companies in particular, there are many stakeholders involved in any large-scale implementation, including (but not limited to) multiple functional departments (i.e., R&D, digital, etc.), brands, regions, legal, finance, and procurement. Navigating this minefield successfully is a difficult but ultimately rewarding task if you can figure it out.

The process for scaling up a pilot to a full implementation is highly specific to the company you are working with, but there are some best practices that can make success more likely.

Understand the Process Up Front

While in the pre-pilot stage, it is critical to ask the questions that are going to be essential to expanding the deal beyond a pilot. Understanding who will need to give their approval, where the budget will come from, who needs to vet the technology, and any other deciding factors are absolutely necessary to get a massive deal done.

To that end, ask your corporate counterpart about the process early on. This will allow you to start building the necessary relationships at an early stage and grow trust over time.

Build Relationships with Everyone You Can Meet

When working with large enterprises, never turn down an opportunity to meet stakeholders and build relationships. Ideally, these meetings will take place in person. As useful as technology is, enterprise deals are orders of magnitude easier when you build in-person relationships.

Along those same lines, any time you get an opportunity to connect with or meet someone from your target company, take it! You never know which stakeholders will be essential to your process. Just as important, building these relationships early on helps build consensus within the company on the merits of working with you. This will pay dividends when it comes time to close a larger deal.

Patience

As you have likely gathered by now, closing deals with large companies is all about the long game. These deals take time . . . lots of it. More than anything else, your best weapon is patience.

CHAPTER 6

MAJOR MISTAKES STARTUPS MAKE WHEN TRYING TO WORK WITH CORPORATE

(And How to Avoid Them)

While the previous chapter discussed the ideal way to handle the corporate sales process, things don't always go according to plan. Sometimes you'll hit a roadblock and the deal will stall. More often than not, this happens because of a mistake you've made.[1] Let's dive into what some of those mistakes could be and how to correct for them. This list is, of course, not exhaustive but is meant to get you in the habit of looking at your own actions and how they might be detrimental to you in the sales process.

MISTAKE #1: Assuming Large Companies Have Limitless Cash (and Other Budget Thoughts)

When pitching to a company the size of Ford, General Electric, Anheuser-Busch, or Google, it's natural to assume that they have wads and wads of cash. In fact, the difference in spending habits of large companies contrasted with the habits of (usually) cash-starved startups couldn't be starker. Those who have been on the inside of a large company know what I'm talking about: car service to get to the airport, hotels, flights, company parties, and more, it all adds up. And just to clarify, I'm not being judgmental here: these are profitable companies, and they can use their money as they wish. That said, all that spending can send a signal to startups that the large company they are selling to is overflowing with cash and can spend an infinite amount of money. This is simply not true.

The key thing to remember here is that you are not selling to the *company* (in the abstract) but instead to an *individual* within that large company. Yes, you may be pitching to a billion-dollar company, but the person you're pitching to doesn't have a billion-dollar budget. In fact, similar to your role as a startup founder or employee, this corporate employee is trying to solve a complex, infinite array of problems with a finite budget. Furthermore, this budget might be even more finite than yours, perhaps not in dollar amount but in flexibility. Corporate budget allocations are usually made on a fiscal-year basis, and shifting money around is pretty much impossible, unless it's being requested by a high-level executive, like someone in the C-suite. For that reason, even if a company is interested in your product or service, timing can play a make-or-break role in whether a deal happens or not.

While corporate budgets may (key word: *may*) have more monetary wiggle room than startup budgets, your corporate counterparts are still dealing with many demands on a limited budget. The importance of knowing whose budget you fit into cannot be overstated. Ultimately, the budget you fall into is your end customer, because if (more like when) that department needs to tighten their belt, they will look at where they can cut spending. Startups often play at the intersections between departments, such as between marketing and technology or between R&D and brand, so fitting into a particular budget can be tricky. Assuming you're at the intersection between just two departments (and not three or more), you'll find that while the two departments are both "interested" in working with you, it will be difficult to get either of them to commit. Each department is essentially waiting on the other one to indicate that they're willing to pay for the service.

The only solution to this problem is to figure out a way to frame your solution as having a specific customer, which means a specific budget. Even if there are tangential customers who derive value from working with you, without a specific budget in place, you'll never get the deal across the finish line.

On top of day-to-day budget concerns, large companies, even successful ones, may implement spending freezes for specific departments. Sometimes this happens because of departmental inefficiency, and other times because of leadership changes. If you're running into roadblocks that don't make much sense, it could be because of a spending freeze; so try to surface that information if you can.

It's also entirely possible that your potential customer will be comparing your product with something in a completely different industry, simply because you're competing for the same budget dollars. For that reason, you need to show why you're not just better than your competitors but that your solution solves a problem of high-enough priority to justify spending their limited budget (and attention) on it.

Conversely, another common startup budget–related issue is not charging *enough* for their product or service. This again comes back to perspective. Startup founders (and humans generally) use their own experience and situation as a framework for the experience of others. There are deep neurological reasons for this (and it relates to the human capability of empathy); but for our current purposes, it's just important to remember that words like "expensive" and "affordable" are relative terms. What's expensive for you as a bootstrapped startup may not be expensive for a large company.

Furthermore, "expensive" is not a term that can be looked at in isolation. Any improvement you bring to your enterprise customer has a scale beyond what it would bring to you. To illustrate, let's assume that your company has a technology that increases revenue per purchase by 1 percent:

Average purchase size: $10

Number of purchases per year: 10,000,000

Total Yearly Revenue: $100,000,000

Revenue per purchase increase: 1 percent

New average purchase size: $10.10

New Total Yearly Revenue: $101,000,000

New Revenue Created by Your Technology: $1,000,000

With this context, would a $300,000-per-year price tag for your technology be considered expensive? Probably not. But if your technology had only created $10,000 in new revenue, of course a $300,000 price tag would be expensive. Context is everything.

By showing some empathy and understanding for the budget concerns of your corporate counterparts, you set yourself apart from other salespeople they encounter and increase the likelihood of closing a deal.

MISTAKE #2: Trivializing Deep Corporate Knowledge

While it is possible that your startup is "changing the world," the Fortune 500 companies you're pitching to have already changed the world and know a thing or two about how things work. There's nothing more annoying to your corporate counterpart than trivializing the deep knowledge they have of their industry.

This is a good time for a caveat: there is immense value in being an outsider. Being an outsider means operating with a different set of assumptions than people in the industry. This is the realm of disruptive innovation.

However, selling into a large company is often less about disruptive innovation and more about how to use what you've created within the broader context of the large company's *system* for mutual benefit. This means that you need the scale of the large company as much as they need the innovation you've created. And creating scale involves industry dynamics that you may not even be aware exist. This is something that startup founders and employees often tend to be brash about, assuming that corporate knowledge is out of date and immaterial to innovation. This is a huge mistake.

There is a deep idea, popularized by Jordan Peterson, author of *12 Rules for Life: An Antidote to Chaos*, about chaos, order, and the line between them. In this context, chaos is where all the assumptions have been thrown out and you have nothing to stand on. This is the "zero" referred to in Peter Thiel's *Zero to One*. Order is a fully defined system: for our purposes, it's a mature company that executes its system and isn't concerned with experimentation. Where true innovation happens, and where we want to be, is where order meets chaos. And that requires both the chaotic innovation of startups and the orderly, methodical systems of large companies. This means you really can't do it alone, no matter how innovative you think your company is.

Most startups are (often by necessity) surer about their assumptions than their data and track record really allow them to be. Do you really think you're the first person to tell a corporate innovation director with twenty years of experience that artificial intelligence is going to take over every industry by 2030? Whether you're right or not, the point is that they've heard that story before and may view your definitive statements as a sign of arrogance. Not helpful in getting a deal done.

There are techniques to balance innovation with respect for corporate knowledge. Phrases like "our hypothesis" when referring to *your* assumptions go a long way toward establishing your honesty and credibility with your corporate counterparts. Humility with respect to the deep industry knowledge held by company insiders is shockingly rarer than you might expect and can help set you apart.

MISTAKE #3: Using Too Much Startup Jargon

True story: the first time I mentioned the word "accelerator" in a corporate R&D lab that I was consulting for, a senior scientist gave me a confused look and said he "didn't realize particle accelerators were funding startups now." While this may initially make you facepalm, it was a great reminder that those of us in "startup world" truly live in a bubble that most of America, and the world, are not part of. Taking the startup jargon down a notch will help you get your point across.

Remember: not everyone reads TechCrunch, follows Naval Ravikant on Twitter, and listens to Tim Ferriss's podcast. It sounds cliché, but knowing your audience is the key to effective communication. When pitching to individuals who've spent their entire careers in large companies, avoid using startup words that they might not understand and connect with. It's not the job of the audience to figure out the presenter—but it is the job of the salesperson to make sure their pitch isn't going over the audience's head.

If you can't avoid certain acronyms in your presentations and discussions—for example, CAC (customer acquisition cost)—you can at least make sure that everyone is on the same page. A good way to do this is to define key acronyms early on in the discussion, not in a patronizing manner but in a way that shows your genuine desire for everyone to understand each other. Conversely, if there are terms that your corporate partner is using that you don't understand, speak up and ask. True story: when I first started Unlimited Brewing, I had no idea what MOQs stood for—it took me months to ask and find out that it stood for Minimum Order Quantity. This is something simple that I would have benefited from asking much sooner.

Acting in a patronizing manner toward your corporate counterpart is a great way to make them feel subtly disrespected: it reduces the probability of getting a deal done. It all comes back to respect: show respect for your corporate counterpart by using vocabulary they'll understand (it's *your* job) and it will pay off by ensuring that your pitch doesn't go right over their heads and into the trash.

MISTAKE #4: Ignoring Implementation Costs

When thinking about how to price your product, it's natural to think that the price *you* set your product at is the cost your customer is going to pay. This, unfortunately for you, is a fallacy. For many large companies, the cost of implementing a new technology often vastly exceeds the cost of the technology itself. And there are many components to implementation cost, such as customer service, training, store layout changes, and more. As an example, let's examine the costs of implementing a new technology inside a company with a large retail footprint.

In the omnichannel world we live in, any large company with a physical retail presence is constantly pitched new in-store technology concepts. While the startups offering these technologies are charging reasonable prices (often as low as $30/location/month), what is often ignored is the cost a company must incur to implement a new technology. For example, a technology that provides customer intelligence via iPad to in-store sales staff so they can sell better requires an extensive training program, troubleshooting, and potentially even in-store hardware upgrades. So even though a technology like this may only cost a total of $6,000 per month (200 locations x $30/location/month), the implementation costs (for things like hardware and training) across 200 locations could easily exceed $100,000.

Implementation costs are difficult to avoid entirely, but there are steps startups can take to help their clients reduce costs and get themselves closer to signing a deal. These steps include negotiating reduced hardware pricing with manufacturers, assisting with or even providing free training, and offering to troubleshoot software issues for sales staff. Whatever you do, the important thing is to make it feasible and simple for the large company to say "yes" to working with you—and that doesn't always involve the price of your actual product.

MISTAKE #5: Spending Too Much Time on the Product and Not Enough on the Problem

This mistake is seen most often in software sales, but it happens in other cases, too. It's an easy mistake to make: we're so excited about the solution we've built that we end up over-focusing on it at the expense of the actual problem we're trying to solve for our corporate partner.

Remember: people only care about your product to the extent that it helps them do something they want to do, such as sell more product or save money. They're generally not that interested in how the product works "under the hood." If your counterpart requests a deeper dive into the product, of course you should spend as much time on it as needed; but jumping into your presentation with the assumption that they care that you used NodeJS to build your product would be a mistake.

Once you're able to snag a meeting with a decision-maker at a large company, it means you've got their attention. They are interested (albeit at a very high level) in what your product can do. That said, these decision-makers are looking at dozens of other companies who are competing for the same budget. The easiest thing for a decision-maker to do is say "no," and making any of the mistakes above gives them an easy out. By always keeping your audience in mind, being empathetic to their concerns, and avoiding critical mistakes, your probability of closing a deal goes way up. And that's ultimately the outcome that both large companies and startup salespeople are after.

MISTAKE #6: Following Up Too Frequently (Being Too Pushy)

Some startup salespeople subscribe to the view that if they just follow up one more time, it'll progress a deal to the next stage. And there is some truth to that. This idea sometimes works because companies don't buy until they are ready to buy; but by frequently following up, you remain top-of-mind for the moment when they are ready to buy. Not a bad strategy.

However, there is a balance to strike. Following up every day while waiting for a company to move forward is clearly not a good idea. You don't want to become annoying. Corporate innovators are human, too; and like all humans, if they dislike someone they won't want to spend time with them and certainly will not want to send business their way, *even if it is in their interest to do so.*

Setting up a regular follow-up cadence is important; but before you start constantly hounding someone, ask yourself what's appropriate. In my experience, following up every three to four weeks for next steps is appropriate, but that interval should be adjusted based on the exact situation. If nothing else, remember this: don't be annoying. It won't get your deal done any faster.

MISTAKE #7: Following Up with the Wrong Person

Sometimes you have a great introductory meeting with a company, but your repeated efforts at following up hit a wall. At that point, it might be worth considering that you might not be speaking with the right person. The tricky thing here is that, on the surface, it may appear that the person is a decision-maker (they probably have an impressive-sounding title); but in reality, they likely don't have the power needed to push your deal through.

Getting to the next person in the hierarchy can be a delicate process. Depending on the individual and their temperament, they may be open to your directly asking them if there are other people involved in the decision. If you can find an informal channel to connecting with some of their colleagues (for example, at an event or through a warm introduction), you'll have a much better chance of learning how the target company's hierarchy works and where your counterpart stands.

MISTAKE #8: Getting Too Emotionally Invested in One Deal and Not Using a Portfolio Approach

Something I have been guilty of as an entrepreneur is getting too overly invested in a single deal. In the previous chapter, I mentioned the value of using a portfolio approach to mitigate the risks of this issue. I can't overstate how vitally important it is.

This mistake is, in general, one of the issues with startups working with large companies. It's not so much about the length of the deal process (six to twelve months or longer), but more about the distraction that these deals can cause. Mitigating this risk requires a disciplined team that won't allow themselves to get jerked around in all kinds of directions at the whim of a large company. Of course, this is easier said than done.

This is why I strongly recommend the portfolio approach when working with large companies. Simply put, make sure you have many irons in the fire. By having many options, not only do you put pressure on your potential partners to speed things up in the deal process, but you also mitigate the risk that you'll get overly invested in any single deal and distract yourself.

Remember: you are building a company, not a product-development shop for a single client.

Dave Knox, author of Predicting the Turn, *co-founder of The Brandery startup accelerator in Cincinnati, and CMO of Rockfish (acquired by WPP), shared his advice on getting overly invested in a single enterprise deal:*

There are a lot of respected VCs that tell their companies to avoid engaging with large companies, especially early on. The first reason for that is when you see the potential of the deal size, you put all your eggs in one basket and the founder is so focused on getting that deal done. And we know that these deals take a long time within corporate and there are a lot of factors that go into that. A founder can waste so much time, money, and effort to get that deal done and can wake up one day and be out of money.

The second issue is treating your enterprise customer as the most important customer, especially when it comes to product feedback. This can effectively turn you into a product-development shop for your corporate partner and stunt your growth.

To read Dave's complete interview, please visit the Appendix.

Conclusion and What's Next

While there are infinitely more errors that you can (and likely will) make while trying to close deals with large organizations, watching yourself for these common errors will help prevent the easy mistakes. Next, we'll take a look at one of the most complex areas of the startup-corporate ecosystem: corporate venture capital.

CHAPTER 7

CORPORATE VENTURE CAPITAL

Golden Ticket, or Deal with the Devil?

It's no secret that startups are considered sexy in the twenty-first century. Thanks to shows like *Shark Tank* and *Silicon Valley* and movies like *The Social Network*, plus the fact that tech titans are dating athletes and actresses, the general public has started viewing startup success in the same way they view Hollywood stars. Okay, maybe startup people aren't *that* cool yet, but it's getting close. Never mind the fact that we've had abnormally low rates of new-business formation in the United States since a high in 2006. More important to our discussion, public *awareness* of what startups bring to the table has never been higher.

Large companies have been taking notice and getting involved in a variety of ways. Much of this book is dedicated to partnership and sales deals with large companies, but another way corporations are getting involved is by investing in startups and having skin in the game for their success. While still only a fraction of total dollars relative to standard venture capital, corporate venture capital has exploded onto the scene in recent years. From 2010 to 2016 alone, corporate venture capital (CVC) dollars as a share of total venture capital dollars grew from 13 percent to 23.5 percent.

Large corporations' desire to participate in the upside of the startups they work with makes complete sense when you take a step back to look at the situation objectively. As we've seen throughout this book, a single massive deal with a large company has the power to transform a startup from "cool project" into a bona fide company. If you wielded that much power, wouldn't you want some of the upside, too? This is essentially a legal form of insider trading. Simply put, if you're about to give a six- or seven-figure deal to a startup, it makes sense to participate in the upside.

There is a major difference between corporate venture capital and standard venture capital, though. While standard venture capital is solely concerned with financial return, corporate venture capital is often motivated by a mixture of two things: strategic value to the corporation, and financial return. In the best examples of corporate venture capital, the CVC group turns into both a profit center for the company *and* a valuable source of innovation akin to R&D. Becoming a profit center is dependent on making smart investments that have a positive return; but being a source of innovation is a bit more straightforward. Developing new technology can be *very* expensive for a large company and is significantly less expensive for startups, for reasons that we will set aside for now. For example, it may cost a large company $50 million to develop a new capability and get it to market. Instead, for $20 million, they can buy a startup working on that same technology—a startup that comes pre-loaded with working technology, a capable team, know-how, and customers. Who would've thought you could rationalize a $20 million acquisition as a bargain? But it's true.

While it's easy to see the strategic and financial value of corporate venture capital on paper, actually executing to deliver and create that value is a whole different animal. There are dozens of different methodologies and ideas on the best way to organize and manage a corporate venture capital group. These range from keeping the entities entirely separate (such as Google Ventures) to being very much integrated into the same company. At the end of the day, it really depends on the company, their culture, and their goals. There is no one-size-fits-all solution for every company.

For startups, this means that you need to evaluate corporate venture capital groups individually, not as a standardized entity type. There are, however, some parameters you can use to evaluate and structure a deal. We'll examine these in detail in this chapter.

Should You Take CVC Money?

Before we get into actual deal structure, let's look at the more important question: Should you take money from a corporate venture capital group? The answer to this, like most difficult questions, is that it depends on a variety of factors.

The Case *for* Taking CVC

There are definitely some good reasons to raise money from corporate venture capital groups. Let's dive in.

Longer Time Horizon Than Traditional Investors

Because corporate venture capital groups typically (though not always) have a dual financial and strategic mandate, they are often more patient with startups. Typical venture capitalists have a sole mandate from their limited partners (LPs—or, in English, the people who invest in VC funds), which is to make a positive financial return—the bigger, the better. While more straightforward, there are some problems with this, especially when it comes to aligning incentives with founders.

Founders (though not all founders) are often interested in building a business with long-term staying power. They have a variety of stakeholders such as employees, customers, investors, and of course themselves. This requires a balancing act on their parts. For example, founders will typically (again not always) not want to screw up their customer relationships for a short-term gain. Ditto with hurting their employees. Investors, on the other hand, usually aren't this noble.

Corporate venture capital is unique as an investor in the sense that, like the founder, they are looking at the business from a long-term-sustainability angle instead of purely as a financial vehicle. If a large company invests in a startup, they are hoping that the startup either becomes a key partner or a subsidiary of the company itself. With that in mind, of course they wouldn't want to screw up all that long-term value for a short-term win. For this reason, CVC can be more patient and, perhaps surprisingly, more founder-aligned than traditional venture capitalists.

Instant Credibility with Your Key Stakeholders

Being a startup can be a slog. Most people don't know you exist; and those that do often don't believe you're as capable as large proven companies. And this perception doesn't just apply to potential customers but also to potential partners, investors, and even employees.

Having a large company as an investor can send a major positive signal that what you're working on is worthwhile. This type of social proof makes complete sense—and we all make use of social proof, whether we know it or not. Why else do companies pay celebrities and influencers millions of dollars to endorse their products? Because Nike (for example) knows that by having a Jordan line of shoes, we (perhaps subconsciously) believe that the shoe will allow us to be "like Mike."

Having a corporate venture capital fund on your cap table has a similar effect. Imagine you're building a self-driving car technology, and General Motors invests in your business. Customers, employees, investors, and partners will instantly believe there is something to your technology because of General Motors' putting cash into the business. And they aren't wrong—CVC funds have a unique perspective on the market, which can elude traditional investors who aren't from the industry.

Strategic Partnerships

Something we've discussed in much detail in this book is the value that large companies can bring to startups via partnerships. Corporate venture capital groups that have dual strategic and financial responsibilities can be extremely useful in making these partnerships come to life. It comes back to skin in the game. When a company has a strong financial incentive to helping you grow, it's in their best interest to do what they can to make that happen. This includes making partnerships work, whether that means help with developing sales channels, or product development, or something else.

Customers

Very often, when a corporate venture capital group is looking to invest in a particular startup, one of the criteria is whether or not the corporation would be a customer of the startup. For example, in *Masters of Corporate Venture Capital* by Andrew Romans, Pär Lange, the managing director of Swisscom Ventures, said: "In my view the ideal case for an investment is when we are able to invest in a company and get Swisscom to become a customer. This means we are doing something good for Swisscom and obviously adding value to the startup."

If a company is about to give a multimillion-dollar customer deal to a startup, it makes sense for them to buy equity in the startup *before* they do the deal. Once the deal is completed, the startup's valuation will increase massively, leading to a near-instant gain for the large company.

The Elephant in the Room: Acquisitions

If you follow the startup world at all, you've seen founders become massively wealthy by selling their startups to large companies. In fact, many of the investors you interact with probably made their money by getting acquired by someone else. In many instances, an investment from a corporate venture capital group can be a prelude to an acquisition by the parent company. This makes complete sense for both sides: it's essentially a tryout to see both if there indeed is a strategic fit *and,* just as important, if the companies' cultures are compatible.

There are a couple of ways that deals can be structured to lead to an acquisition—either explicitly or implicitly defined. One thing that is absolutely crucial to understand, however, is that not every investment will lead to an acquisition. And this is actually one of the hidden risks of taking corporate venture capital money. More on that below.

The Case Against CVC

Unfortunately, CVC isn't all sunshine and rainbows. There are some downsides, too, which we'll take a look at below.

Conflicts of Interest

Depending on how much of a stake you sell to a CVC, there is a strong possibility that your traditional investors and your CVC will have misaligned incentives. This can lead to some major issues down the road. Imagine you have given up a significant stake plus a board seat to a CVC in one of your fund-raising rounds. At a later date, a competitor of your CVC's parent company comes around and is interested in purchasing your startup for a massive amount of money. Unfortunately, your CVC is really not into this idea, while you and your other investors are thrilled. Depending on the terms of the CVC investment, they may be able to block this rival from acquiring your company, even if everyone else is in agreement.

Furthermore, by taking CVC money, you open yourself up to conflicts of interest between yourself and the parent company. This can happen predictively, if you compete with the large company or are a disruptive threat to their business, or in completely unexpected ways. For example, in 2017, Amazon acquired Whole Foods in a $13.7 billion acquisition. What went unnoticed (or little noticed) at the time was that Whole Foods was an investor in the grocery delivery company Instacart. While their exact stake hasn't been publicly disclosed (at least as of this writing), this presents some problems for Instacart because Amazon has a competing grocery delivery service. By all accounts, Whole Foods was a great partner for Instacart, helping with both awareness and customer acquisition. But it's unclear if that will remain with Amazon at the helm, though I highly doubt the partnership will be as fruitful moving forward.

This is a risk you open yourself up to when accepting money from a CVC. After all, there is no risk that one of your financial VCs will be acquired by a competitor.

Overvaluation

I imagine you're raising your eyebrows at overvaluation being listed as a negative side of corporate venture capital. I can assure you, however, that overvaluation can be a curse disguised as a blessing. I had a hard time believing this until reading a Medium post[1] by Innovation Works' investor Dave Lishego, which elaborated on this point brilliantly. Take the following hypothetical scenario, which I have crafted using the principles presented in Dave's article:

You are raising a $6M Series B round, and the largest company in your industry is enamored with you. They offer to not only lead the round, but to invest the entire $6M you are looking for, and that, too, at a $60M valuation. You've had conversations with other investors, and it seems they would only invest at a $30M valuation. You're obviously going to go with the CVC, right? Not so fast. What happens if the CVC has a leadership change in eighteen months and is no longer so thrilled about working with startups, right as you are ready to raise your Series C? Now you have no lead investor, your valuation is too high, and your main corporate partner/potential acquirer walked away. Good luck closing that Series C, buddy.

This risk is exactly why you need to be cautious about valuations and the VCs you work with. Higher valuation is not always better.

Negative Signaling

This is industry-specific, but certain large companies have developed negative reputations over the years within their industry. You as the founder need to weigh whether it's worth being affiliated with a large company who has a negative industry rep in exchange for the value they are bringing to the table. Their negative reputation may cut you off from future opportunities with customers, partners, and acquirers. It could be worth it . . . or it might not be. You'll have to evaluate this on a case-by-case basis, but it is definitely something to keep in mind.

Right of First Refusal Clauses

As part of an investment, some CVCs will try to include a "right of first refusal" clause that allows them to see all acquisition offers and have the right to match or outbid the would-be acquirer. While this might initially seem innocuous, it may effectively *prevent* any competitor to your CVC from even making a bid for your company. That means you're not going to be able to get two (or more) competitors involved in a bidding war with each other for the rights to your technology. As you may be aware, a bidding war is great for driving valuation upwards— and is something your non-CVC investors are hoping for.

With that context in mind, it makes perfect sense that a large company would want to sneak this clause into the deal. It effectively means they can sit and wait until the perfect moment for them to acquire your company. If they ever even do it. This is not good news for you, and it's a major reason why you should avoid this clause if at all possible.

CVC Too Early in the Startup Life Cycle

Another risk for startups working with CVCs is that the sheer size of the CVC will overwhelm them. For example, if a seed-stage startup takes money from a CVC who is also becoming a customer, it is highly likely that this single corporate customer will make up 50 percent or more of the startup's revenue. This is a dangerous position to be in, for a couple of reasons. One, the large company knows that they have leverage with you: if they stop working with you, 50 percent of your revenue vanishes. And two, perhaps less maliciously, you run the risk that your startup could become a product-development shop for the large company. Understandably, you will pay attention to the features your customer and investor are requesting. If this happens too early in the company's life cycle, it's easy to accidentally build a product that is *too* customized and only solves your corporate partner's needs.

The Verdict

So, where does that leave us? Should you, or shouldn't you, deal with corporate venture capitalists? The answer isn't clear: it depends more on what you're trying to accomplish. If the CVC that approaches you is the only logical acquirer for your company, then perhaps the risk isn't so great. On the other hand, you run the risk of cutting yourself off from options.

CVC, like most other strategic decisions, is a calculated risk. Tread carefully.

Dave Knox, author of Predicting the Turn, *co-founder of The Brandery startup accelerator in Cincinnati, and CMO of Rockfish (acquired by WPP), shared some thoughts on startups taking money from corporate venture capital groups:*

I see an almost equal number of pros and cons for taking corporate venture capital. So if I were a startup, I would ask myself why the corporate is getting involved and what stage they typically get involved at.

It's really important to look at the potential downside, too. This can happen if the company is just too early or, alternatively, if the large company's competitors won't engage with you simply because you have taken an investment from one of their rivals. That could make things really tricky very fast.

It's really easy to see all the positives of working with a large corporate partner, but as the CEO, it's important to pay attention to the downside also.

To read Dave's full interview, please visit the Appendix.

CVC Deal Structures

Assuming you're going to work with a corporate venture capital group, there are many ways a deal can be optimally structured. Structuring the deal the right way can help mitigate some of the risks outlined above with CVC. And conversely, if you structure the deal the wrong way, you're doomed before you even get started.

Traditional Investment

In this format, the corporate venture capital group behaves like any other investor. To be honest, there aren't too many corporate investors like this, even though many claim to be. It just isn't easy for corporate money to be allocated in a purely financial manner while completely ignoring the strategic side of things. However, Google Ventures and Intel Capital are two of the best examples of this type of structure.

For more on traditional investment structures, I strongly recommend reading *Venture Deals* by Brad Feld and Jason Mendelson.

Traditional Investment with Caveats

Similar to standard traditional investments, but this time there's a catch. For example, a company may want to include a "right of first refusal" clause, which effectively means any potential acquirer will need to be approved by them. This is an extremely dangerous clause and one to watch out for. As an attorney once told me, "Startups who allow the right of first refusal clause are basically selling their company for $250K" (or whatever amount they are raising from the large company). The reason for this is that if one of the large company's competitors offers to buy your company, they can be (and usually will be) turned down by your corporate "partner." For most companies, that means you're out of options and can only sell to your original corporate partner, preventing a bidding war that could have greatly aided your valuation.

Another potential catch that large companies can throw into the deal is exclusivity. Similar to the right of first refusal, except that in this case you can't even work with any of their competitors. Talk about cutting off your options.

Be wary of the strings attached to the investment dollars thrown your way by corporate venture capitalists.

Investment with Option to Buy

While more common for later-stage companies, this type of investment occurs when the corporate investor has a very clear interest in acquiring the company they are investing in. Very often, this type of investment will be a significant stake with a clause tied in that allows the corporate to buy the rest of the shares at a pre-agreed price by a certain date.

Typically, this type of deal will be used when there is a very difficult technology being developed, for example in the pharmaceutical industry. The acquisition clause will be related to a stage of the drug-development process that will only be exercised if the startup passes a certain hurdle (since by passing the hurdle, their valuation will be higher than the strike price of the option).

Joint Venture

In this type of collaboration, the startup and the corporate effectively form a new company together. This makes the most sense when the startup is working with the large company to enter a market completely different from the one it normally operates in. Furthermore, the startup would likely have no intention of entering this market. Of course, this type of arrangement works best when the startup has some proprietary technology or process.

A joint venture can also be just a fancy form of partnership, where there is no new company formed to tackle the opportunity.

For a large company, a joint venture may be a way of acquiring a technology without acquiring a company. Having spent two and a half years with The Estée Lauder Companies looking for technologies outside the industry, I know that there are some amazing collaboration opportunities hidden in seemingly random industries. If a large company comes across a startup in a completely different field with a technology that's applicable to their industry, it doesn't need to acquire the whole company: it just needs to buy the rights to the technology within their particular industry. The large company will of course have to pay for this privilege, and likely will also have to pay a royalty on sales. This can work very nicely for both sides. The startup gets an up-front cash payment (all of us in the startup world know how damn valuable cash is, especially in the early days) and a stake in the upside, while the large company gets access to a new technology with rights to everything relevant to them. Furthermore, the large company gets rights to a technology that they likely couldn't have developed internally, since it may be outside their field of expertise.

Conclusion

While it is impossible to say with certainty whether or not you should take money from corporate venture capital groups, looking at the decision through the lens of these pros and cons will allow you to make the most objective decision.

Next, we'll take a look at some examples of startup and corporate interactions, examining some case studies as well as specific emails to demonstrate the right and wrong ways to interact with companies.

3

CREATING
A BETTER
CORPORATE
INNOVATION
ECOSYSTEM FOR
EVERYONE

CHAPTER 8

THE BEST AND WORST OF STARTUP-CORPORATE INTERACTIONS

So far, much of what I've discussed and recommended has been abstract (those in corporate would call this "best practices"). In this chapter, we'll be exploring some specific examples to learn how to appropriately interact and negotiate with large companies. As we'll see, this is especially relevant when deals get stalled or things get stuck in the back office, such as with accounting or legal. Your skill in these interactions can also be of crucial importance when working through the deal terms and details of a potential relationship or partnership.

Dave Knox, author of Predicting the Turn, *co-founder of The Brandery startup accelerator in Cincinnati, and CMO of Rockfish (acquired by WPP), shared his advice on getting overly invested in a single enterprise deal:*

(continued on next page)

(continued from previous page)

A really good example of a deal where there was a win-win on both sides is when Caterpillar invested in (and later acquired) Yard Club. For Yard Club, the investment didn't really cut them off from any future options with other companies in the industry. Meanwhile, Caterpillar was able to explore and study this peer-to-peer lending model to see if there was any merit to it before making a big bet.

The TechStars Disney program is particularly interesting to me. We had one of our Brandery companies go through their accelerator—the company is FamilyTech. The company had already raised a Series A and about half the companies in the accelerator had raised a Series A, or beyond—so clearly not a typical accelerator. Our company came into the accelerator with the clear goal that they wanted to collaborate. One of the tangible things that came out of that collaboration was the BB8 Robot, which a couple years ago was Disney's top-selling holiday toy. That's what can happen when these collaborations are done right.

To read Dave's complete interview, please visit the Appendix.

The examples below are real-world examples of how to (and how not to) deal with issues as they arise in startup-corporate interactions and negotiations.

Troubleshooting Examples

Deal Stalling in Procurement

If you plan on selling to corporate, there is no doubt that you will face issues with back-office departments like accounting, procurement, and legal. Procurement can especially be a difficult area for a startup to navigate, since the process is normally built for companies much larger than yours. There is a tasteful way to resolve these conflicts. Let's take a look:

> Hi, [Name Redacted],
>
> I'm writing in the hopes you may have some ideas to get our contract through. . . .
>
> We're over a month in with [Procurement Person] and haven't been able to make any real progress on the agreement. During that time we spent several hundred in legal fees on markup, in the hopes of expediting the process, almost all of which [Procurement Person] has asked us to remove in order to get it through at legal. Even after doing so, it's been over 2 weeks since I've heard any sign of progress, and have no clear sense of next steps.
>
> I know you guys had wanted to kick off the pilot in the summer. We are already well into a sufficient time frame to do so. At this rate, who knows when we'll actually get any work started. Has the intended start date changed?
>
> I appreciate any thoughts or guidance on the matter. We'd be happy to set up a quick call if you'd like to discuss options.
>
> Thanks,
>
> [Name Redacted]

This email is a brilliant method of solving issues with procurement. The first thing that stands out is that it's forceful yet polite. It also won't be taken lightly, as it pretty clearly states that the requested time line for a pilot is already going to be difficult.

The time-line callout is an important one. What startup teams often miss when interacting with large companies is the fact that each silo within the large company has different needs. The team signing off (and paying for) the work with the startup in the email example is hiring the startup to solve a specific need. This need seems to have a summer time line. However, the procurement department doesn't have that same summer time line. For them, the only goal is getting the contract done without any risk whatsoever. So that means they will go through their normal rules and procedures, without any regard for time line or who the contractor is.

By communicating procurement's lack of urgency with the buyer, the startup raises alarm bells with the person who really cares about (and is judged on) the time line. The buyer will now put pressure on procurement to speed up, perhaps even enlisting the help of senior management if necessary. And in turn, this can actually speed up procurement's time line for one simple reason: procurement is not a profit center. They are a service to the rest of the company, and they are ultimately being paid by the rest of the company, in particular the profit centers. As such, pressure from senior management works really well to speed up procurement. The same principle applies to groups like accounting, accounts payable, etc.: they respond really well to pressure from senior management.

The final thing I want to mention about this well-worded email is the emphasis on legal costs. As I've mentioned elsewhere, many of the issues on the corporate side of these startup-corporate interactions come from a simple lack of awareness. By giving your corporate partner visibility into the problems you're experiencing and the hardship they are causing, you make them aware and able to correct the issues. Most of the corporate partners you encounter are interested in creating a productive long-term relationship and will work to remove these obstacles once they are aware that they exist.

Miscommunications and the Maze of Corporate Responsibilities

The email below highlights the complex array of responsibilities in corporate back offices. This is another issue that can occur often with projects that don't fit neatly into an existing bucket. Since startups and innovative projects tend to exist at the edges or intersections of corporate departments, this issue happens more than you might expect.

Hey, [Name Redacted],

I hope you're having a great week so far!

It looks like there was a miscommunication with [Name Redacted], and he's actually not able to/responsible for signing contracts—he had only been enrolling me in [Company]'s system the last couple of weeks.

I spoke with [Name Redacted] and it seems like sending a contract to procurement is a slow process. I don't want to hold things up on this project—but I also don't want to start things without a signed contract.

The contract I use is an industry-standard contract that freelance designers use; it's open-sourced online and thousands of designers use it. The only changes I made to the contract were to add my name as the contractor, [Company] as the client, and some basic details about project scope and cost.

Do you know if there is any way to move the contract-signing process along that wouldn't require waiting for the procurement team?

And if procurement is the only option, how does that affect the project time line on your end? I have the contract attached for your reference, along with the accompanying proposal (some references are made from one to the other, although only the contract requires a signature).

Thanks for your advice and help with this! Eager to hear your thoughts.

[Name Redacted]

Once again, this is a great example of effective troubleshooting. There was a clear miscommunication of the process by the corporate team; but instead of getting angry or blaming them for things, this individual calmly offered an alternative.

Most importantly, the freelancer explained why the alternative they are suggesting is not a risky one. The importance of this can't be overemphasized. Any time you circumvent an established process, the risk is that your corporate counterpart (or other people within the organization) will freak out and put a stop to it. By preemptively mentioning that the contract you've attached is a completely standard one, as well as calling out the only changes you've made, there is a much lower chance of anyone panicking about the change in standard procedure.

Again, just like in the first example, this person also made sure to emphasize the project time line and did so in a subtle, yet clear, manner. Instead of saying angrily that procurement is going to cause a delay with their process, this person made clear that, in the interest of time, they'd like to find a way forward without working with procurement. Furthermore, this is framed as being to corporate's benefit ("I don't want to hold things up on this project").

Negotiation Examples

Like any contract, closing a deal with a large company is a negotiation. We've talked about many of the important deal terms in earlier chapters, but now we'll see how it's all put together using simple real-world scenarios.

Simple Price Negotiation

You're working on getting your software implemented within the R&D department of a large company, called Acme Inc. Your software typically costs $1,000 per month per user, but typically you sell subscriptions individually. With Acme's R&D department, you have the opportunity to sell forty subscriptions at once! What a game-changing opportunity... if you can close it.

Acme is understandably worried about the $40,000-per-month price tag if they implement your software throughout the entire department. Being cognizant of this issue, you are open to giving a discount of up to 25 percent per user. However, coming right out and giving this discount is surprisingly the wrong move here.

A better way to play this would be to offer the discount *if* Acme is willing to pay you yearly. This means that instead of paying $40,000 per month, they would pay you a lump sum of $360,000 for the whole year, paid at the start of the contract.

As I hope I've made clear throughout this book, a dollar has a very different *relative* value to startups versus corporates. For cash-poor startups, dollars in the bank today are incredibly valuable. While monthly recurring contracts are nice, bringing in revenue up front for the year instead of monthly allows the startup to invest in new features, recruiting new team members, and marketing to grow the business even further. In contrast, large companies have the luxury of cash on their balance sheets. Cash, while valuable, is simply not the most important factor to large companies when entering into these negotiations.

This brings us to another relevant point in these negotiations: the time horizon that startups use is different than what large companies use. Typically, large organizations (and the employees who work for them) are evaluated on at least a quarterly—but more often annual—basis. This means that the cost of a deal to them will be annualized, whether or not you are billing them monthly or annually. So by getting paid up front, you—the startup—are getting something of value, while your corporate partner might not be giving up anything. This can be a difficult point for people with only startup experience to understand: your corporate counterpart is likely not thinking about anything from a monthly standpoint. So even if you frame your pricing as a monthly cost and even if you bill your customer monthly, it is extremely likely that they are annualizing the cost.

For corporate innovators, payment terms are a very useful negotiating point. By making these terms more favorable for the startup (now that you know cash is king), you can then negotiate for other terms in exchange. Once again, there is a path to creating win-win deals. You just need to use a little empathy to get there.

Exclusivity Negotiation

While the pricing example above was fairly straightforward, things can get a bit trickier when special terms like exclusivity are involved. Some companies negotiate these terms in a blanket manner—for example, they may have a policy to always negotiate for exclusivity of some sort, such as industry exclusivity. Others negotiate these terms on a case-by-case basis.

For companies with a technology that applies to many different industries, it is typically a bad idea to sell *global exclusivity* to anyone. By selling global[1] exclusivity, you are essentially signing your company (or, at the very minimum, that technology) away, since you would be prohibited from selling it to anyone else. There are few instances where selling global exclusivity makes sense, but a distinct one that comes to mind is if your startup develops a "side" technology or capability that is outside your core business. In those instances, it might make sense to sell exclusive rights. Just make sure the price is worth it.

However, more common than global exclusivity is a negotiation for *industry exclusivity*. If you have a technology that spans multiple industries, this term can be a powerful one for you to wield and dangle as a carrot, especially once you have some early traction. Effectively, what you're saying is: "This technology that you know works so well can be locked up and used exclusively by you. But if not, your competitor will be using it next week." Whenever exclusivity is discussed, there is a bit of an implicit threat that both sides are cognizant of in the discussion. For startups, one of the best things about negotiating for industry exclusivity is that it can be sold to multiple industries. Or you can sell exclusivity in industries you have no interest in playing in yourself, while still pursuing industries you are more comfortable with.

While there are as many different styles of exclusivity negotiations as there are deals, one commonality is that the rights holder (the startup) receives some form of compensation in exchange for the exclusivity. This compensation can come in the form of a payment (onetime or, more commonly, recurring) but can also include items like resources, co-branding, or even infrastructure investment. While exclusivity negotiations can be tricky, they also allow for much creativity.

Disclosure Negotiation

One of the most important benefits of working with large companies (besides cash from the deal) is the social proof that their logos give you. Having the logo of a well-respected brand on your website is a stamp of approval that will not only further fuel your customer lead funnel but also grab the attention of future employees, partners, and investors. That said, some large companies are very protective of their brands and will be hesitant to allow you to broadcast your relationship to the wider world.

This deal term has a bit of a dual nature to it. As discussed earlier, there is a positive benefit to being associated with "innovation" and startups. The companies that recognize this are more likely to agree to—or even encourage—press efforts around making their startup collaborations well known. These companies may issue their own press releases, and some have even gone so far as to mention startup collaborations in their annual reports or earnings calls with analysts. The companies that do this know that there is a benefit to their brand (and their stock price) for being affiliated with innovative technology.

That said, in spite of this, there is still a strong contingent of companies that will hesitate to allow startups to broadcast their relationship. As annoying as this can be to startup founders (particularly after all the effort it takes to close a deal in the first place), there is some logic to this. The first and most important reason is that, barring an acquisition, large companies can't control your actions. If tomorrow your startup is involved in some major scandal and is publicly affiliated with the large company, the scandal will tarnish their brand by association. This is an unfortunate side effect of how human brains operate, but large companies know how important brand (aka reputation) is and how expensive it is to build. But more importantly, they know how easy that reputation is to destroy. Affiliating their brand with a startup—which, let's face it, usually doesn't have strict guidelines on hiring rules or employee relationships, and is often just flying by the seat of its pants—can be a risk they just don't want to deal with. And can you really blame them?

As a startup in need of social proof and press, you should do your best to make sure that you're allowed to broadcast your relationship with this large company far and wide. New relationships with large companies will often get the attention of the press, particularly industry press. As we know, people tend to be followers, not leaders, and will wait until there are other companies working with you before they make their move. In addition, investors, potential employees, and other stakeholders will feel more comfortable that what you're building has real potential.

However, the one time you may want to be careful with press is if there is any negative sentiment surrounding the large company you are working with. If their reputation will prevent you from doing future deals, you may find the situation reversed and experience the large company negotiating with *you* for the right to broadcast their new relationship.

Like every other deal term we've discussed so far, disclosure of your relationship with a large company is a term that can be negotiated. While I wouldn't lead the discussion with this topic, "disclosure" is a term to bring up once it becomes apparent that a deal is going to happen. You may find that your corporate partner is open to this term but in exchange will want the right to approve any press release that goes out mentioning the partnership. While your exact circumstances will vary, this is a term that seems tolerable.

Conclusion and What's Next

While not exhaustive, I hope these examples have shed light on the nature of negotiations with large companies (and of negotiation in general). It is all a give-and-take. Each party—you and your corporate partner—has a set of goals they are trying to accomplish, with varying priorities. The negotiation is a way to find the acceptable intersection between each party's set of priorities.

Startup founders in particular have an obligation to be strong negotiators. Remember—large companies aren't doing you a favor by interacting and working with you: they are using your capabilities as a means to an end. As the larger party, they often have (or at least act like they have) the leverage in the negotiation. But this oversimplifies the nature of startup-corporate interactions. By virtue of the fact that they're negotiating, it means you have something coveted that they don't have, despite their resource advantage. Otherwise, they wouldn't even be speaking with you. So when negotiating and interacting with large companies, be strong, be bold, and demand terms that you believe are fair.

Next, we'll dive into the inevitable problems you'll have to deal with when your corporate innovators make a mistake, whether that means getting caught up in back-office hell to get a deal approved or simply forgetting to pay you.

CHAPTER 9

WHAT TO DO WHEN CORPORATE INNOVATORS SCREW UP

(And How to Avoid These Mistakes)

Like all human beings, corporate innovators are not infallible. In your interactions with corporate innovators, there will be miscommunications, screw-ups, and mistakes along the way. Rest assured that these mistakes are usually not malicious: instead, they are simply problems associated with living in a different reality. As we discussed in detail earlier, people in corporate are speaking a different language, are judged on different metrics, and have different time horizons than their startup brethren.

A common (and perhaps all too familiar) example is a startup that is relying on a big contract for much-needed cash flow. The terms are agreed to, the contract is signed, and the deal appears to be wrapped up. Everything is groovy, right? Not so fast . . . you still need to get paid. And thanks to Murphy's Law, the corporate accounting department will screw up exactly when you need them to pay you on time. And as we said, it's not necessarily malicious (unless you subscribe to the view that the Universe is inherently trying to get in your way—which I don't), but there will be some weird coincidence such as a key employee who is out on vacation or an email that slipped through the cracks.

Other types of issues can occur along the way to closing a deal, often through no direct fault of your own. Something as simple as getting on the calendar of all the decision-makers can delay the progress of a deal by a month or more (shocking to those who have never worked in corporate, while those readers who are corporate veterans are nodding their heads in agreement). Or sometimes your internal champion (more on that crucial individual below) will be delayed by an urgent priority that takes up their attention.

While these miscommunications and screw-ups will inevitably occur, there are a number of things you can do to reduce their frequency and magnitude. This chapter is a guide to preventing, troubleshooting, and generally solving corporate screw-ups, with an eye toward continuing to move your deal forward. Let's dive in.

SCREW-UP #1: Speaking Out of Turn

In your search for a strong internal champion, you're likely to home in on an ambitious individual who is genuinely trying to do their best to bring innovative new solutions into their company. Taking us back to chapter 2 of this book, this type of individual is usually classified as the Corporate Striver or the Startup Wannabe. And like many ambitious individuals (and perhaps in true startup fashion), they will sometimes make promises they can't keep. A common example, particularly for the Corporate Striver, is they will often act as if they have more power than they actually have—or even as if they are the final decision-maker.

For this reason, it's extremely important to get the lay of the land as early as possible in the conversation. Some questions that will help you do that include:

- Which department in the company is typically responsible for paying for products/services/technologies like ours?
- Who ultimately decides on whether or not to move forward on projects similar to ours?
- What does the process look like between here and hypothetically implementing a project together?
- Is there anything we can provide you with that would make the process easier?
- Assuming there is mutual interest in moving forward, what does the time line look like?

Of course, asking these questions won't give you a perfect sense of who you need to be talking to and how the process works, but it will certainly be better than flying blind. Just as importantly, it will allow you to quickly sniff out whether or not you are speaking to a decision-maker. Even though a Corporate Striver might be ambitious, they will rarely lie and claim that they are a decision-maker when they aren't.

A word of warning for startups: a very common trap, one which I have fallen into plenty of times, is to get overly excited when you seem to have interest from a large company—whether that is for a partnership, customer relationship, or acquisition. The biggest mistake is to take your eye off the ball—to divert

(continued on next page)

(continued from previous page)

from your strategy—simply because you have interest from a large company. Most of the time, these types of conversations with corporate don't go anywhere, not because of something you're doing wrong, but because you aren't speaking with a decision-maker. I've especially noticed this issue with founders who haven't worked in corporate. It's easy to get impressed by a Director or Vice President title; but those who have spent time in corporate know that most large companies have hundreds of Directors and (at least) dozens of Vice Presidents in various departments and groups. Title inflation is real.

That said, even if you are speaking with the decision-maker, it's extremely important to continue pushing on with what's working, and not get distracted by the corporate interest.

SCREW-UP #2: Committing to a Deal Term Before Checking with the Back Office

An important distinction that is missed by many of us on the startup side of the table is that we are often interacting with individuals in roles like "New Business Development" or "Innovation." These people are trained to find ways to say "yes." It is in their best interest to get deals done and bring new technologies, products, services, and ultimately revenue or cost savings to their company. What most of us miss, however, is that even when we get a "yes" from the business decision-maker, there is still a whole other chasm to cross: the back office.

The back office is a group made up of legal, accounting, supply chain, and other groups who have a crucial but sometimes annoying (for our purposes) goal: removing and managing risk for the large company. And, unfortunately, working with a startup can be a huge potential risk for a large company.

Here's a classic example: when speaking with a corporate innovator about how a deal could work, you (the startup founder) may ask if you can put out a press release about your new project with large company X and include their logo on your website. This would be great for your company—press, customers, investors, and potential employees will view the new relationship with the large company as a sign of your momentum and inevitable rise. Most of the time, your corporate counterpart won't have any issue with this—after all, it doesn't cost her anything to say yes to this request, and it helps you out. However, problems arise when this request makes its way to the back office. Legal will want to put some type of nondisclosure clause into the contract.

This is a crucial thing to note: legal isn't doing this because they want to be party-poopers. They are doing this to de-risk the situation for the company. How so, you might ask. There are many reasons, but one that isn't exactly a secret is that startups have a high degree of variance with their internal culture and corporate governance. As we've seen in recent years with startups like Uber, startup cultures can often get out of control. By being publicly affiliated with a particular startup, a large company runs the risk of having its reputation damaged by association, through no fault of its own. One of the roles of the back office is to prevent situations like this. Hence the request for a nondisclosure clause in the contract. This doesn't mean that you can never get around a nondisclosure clause or that legal will never budge on that deal term, but simply that your counterpart in innovation or new business development can't really speak on this deal term with authority.

Another issue that can pop up frequently with business-side promises and back-office backtracking is payment terms. During my time in corporate, I was a big advocate for using up-front and startup-friendly payment terms. For example: don't make the startup pay out of pocket for anything, front-load payments when possible, and increase cash payments while reducing royalty or residual payments. The reason for this is simply that large companies are cash-rich and startups are cash-poor. It makes sense—for both parties—for large companies to use that cash to their advantage. However, this is another area where it's easy for a corporate innovator to speak out of turn (as I did on occasion). Accounting usually has its own rules for payment terms, and changing those can be like pulling teeth: extremely painful. The only way a corporate innovator can make this happen (despite what they may promise) is if they have "air cover" from a high-level executive, ideally someone in the C-Suite.[1] Otherwise, it's very, very likely that accounting will block this request or drag their feet so much as to not make this worth it for anyone.

While the examples are endless, all these issues come down to risk. And while innovators—both startup and corporate—are accustomed to risk, back-office employees are not. It's also worth remembering that anything new is risky. There are no procedures, processes, or examples to draw on—which is not what a back-office employee is used to. Finally, as much as I know how dangerous it can be to generalize, it's difficult to picture a swashbuckling, risk-loving corporate attorney or accountant.

My recommendation here is that once you have buy-in from your corporate counterpart on any deal terms that involve the back office, you ask them if they can organize a conversation with the relevant back-office team members. Make sure you are included. If your corporate counterpart has to pitch these terms to the back office on their own, it's all but guaranteed that they won't get approved. Instead, join the meeting and make your best case for why these terms are needed, how they help the large company, and what you're willing to give up in exchange for these beneficial terms.

SCREW-UP #3: Legal Roadblocks

Like most back-office employees, lawyers, God bless them, are in the business of reducing risk for their employer. Understanding that their objectives are very different from both your objectives *and* the objectives of your corporate counterpart is the key to understanding why they care so much about certain things that you didn't even know existed.

One thing lawyers are often overly cautious about is definitions. You may think certain things are self-explanatory, but that's because you aren't a lawyer. For example, if a lawyer is negotiating industry exclusivity, they will be very careful about how they define their industry. The definition they will want to include will be broad. It's in *your* interest for the definition to be straightforward and narrow. This is something you'll have to negotiate.

Another area lawyers will pay a lot of attention to is exit strategy. In the interest of risk mitigation, lawyers will be concerned about how things will play out if the deal goes south and the relationship between their company and yours needs to be terminated. This can put a damper on the "happily ever after" vibe that you and your corporate counterpart may have developed during the negotiation of business terms. But a better way to think about this is as a pre-nup[2]—it's a deal term you'd rather negotiate up front than to not have it when you need it. This is especially true when dealing with large companies, since they can out-litigate you by many, many orders of magnitude. Depending on the exact nature of your deal, you may want to include terms like a breakup fee, return of IP, a non-compete clause, and even a non-solicitation clause (meaning they can't poach your employees).

A very common way that deals get derailed is that you get buy-in from your corporate counterpart, who then sends the deal "to legal." Given the way this very often plays out, it might as well be referred to as sending the deal to a black hole. In my experience, I'd recommend playing this a different way. Keeping your corporate counterpart directly involved in all conversations with legal is very important. I can't emphasize this enough. When deals are being discussed and examined through a purely legal lens, the main factor determining how to move forward is risk. This is not good—especially for you, the risky startup. Instead, when your internal champion is involved, the deal is examined with an eye to getting the deal consummated—while mitigating risk. It's a completely different attitude, and one that provides the deal with the momentum to reach completion.

And a note to corporate innovators: this type of screw-up can be very financially damaging to startups, as they very rarely have in-house counsel. Dragging them into legal dogfights over ultimately minimally important deal terms can severely damage your relationship before it even gets started. Smart corporations will take this as an opportunity to leapfrog their competitors. By building a more startup-friendly path to reaching agreement on deal terms, you'll build a great reputation and greatly improve both your deal flow and close rate.

SCREW-UP #4: Payment Delays

Of all the possible screw-ups, this one is probably my biggest pet peeve. This is the one that feels the most superfluous. The deal is completed, everyone is (hopefully) happy, the contract is signed, and you're ready to roll. You're just waiting for the first payment and you'll get started. In fact, you're so excited that you get started before you even receive the first payment to kick off the project. On the day that the first payment is supposed to arrive, you eagerly check your bank account—and there's no payment. No worries, you think: the payment probably takes a couple of days to show up. You check the next day, and the day after that, and the day after that—still no payment. At this point, you start to get worried and contact your corporate counterpart. Since it's a Friday (remember Murphy's Law?), they say that they'll check with accounting on Monday. On Monday, you find out that accounting never sent you the forms (like a W-4) to get added to the payment system, leading to another two- or three-week delay. This type of screw-up happens so often, it's hard to even call it a screw-up. It might as well be part of the process. And it will give you recurring nightmares, especially if you're relying on revenue to fund your business.

Even worse, though these delays in payment might technically be violations of the contract, you have little recourse. After all, are you really going to sue your corporate partner for late payment? You'd have to be out of your mind.

The only way I've ever seen to solve this is to preemptively try to get ahead of the problem. This includes asking your corporate counterpart to put you in contact with Accounts Payable (or whoever the department is that is in charge of paying you). Once in contact with the appropriate individual, you *must* proactively ask if there are any forms you need to fill out or information you need to provide to the department that will expedite the payment process. Usually, this is enough to get the process moving. Remember, the delays in payment are not malicious in nature—they are simply a side effect of a large bureaucracy. And ultimately, as important as you feel your startup is, it is an extremely small project relative to what the large company is already working on. Your corporate customer may owe you a $5,000 project kick-off payment; but relative to the rest of their payments, this might not even be a drop in the bucket. A better analogy is that your payment is more like a water molecule in the ocean.

The Way Forward—How Large Companies Can Better Structure the Back Office for Startup/ Corporate Success

While everything discussed in this chapter so far has been in relation to how most companies have set up their front- and back-office structures, I'll now share my personal recommendations for how large companies can structure their back office to improve the odds of success for their deals with startups.

Build a Fast Track

Startup deals are fundamentally different from other types of deals. The needs are different, the goals are different, and the re-sources are different. Traditional deal structures and back-office procedures are often built with an inherent assumption, namely that both entities are sizeable companies with resources and lawyers.

To get around this issue, I recommend that large companies build a separate workflow to handle deals with startups. This workflow should be built for the customer, which in this case includes both the corporate innovator tasked with working with startups, and of course the startups themselves. This has been done well by companies like P&G.

Arden Rosenblatt, founder of PieceMaker Technologies, an innovative startup developing additive manufacturing and 3D printing solutions for companies across industries, on what he views to be one of the most difficult aspects of working with large companies:

The hardest part of working with a large company, for startups, is that the timetables are extremely long. Small companies often do not have the resources to develop robust sales pipelines and portfolios of leads, which means that many can bleed out waiting on large first contracts to hit. I'm not sure if corporate partners always realize that this is a real constraint for small companies and startups.

In many ways, startups operate more like a private contractor than a large corporation. Every project they undertake is critical to cash flow, and they schedule very tightly to meet those opportunities they see as best. Working with large companies involves inevitable delays as project teams try to secure all the approvals and input associated with safely bringing new products to market. If companies understood the extent to which this can bleed out a smaller company, there may be room to streamline the process, in turn providing more security to startups, likely lowering prices and improving rates of success.

To read Arden's complete interview, please visit the Appendix.

While the exact nature of your corporate fast track will depend on your industry and your culture, here are some elements to keep in mind:

Shorter NDA Process

Let's face it: NDAs are notoriously difficult to enforce, and spending three months negotiating one is a colossal waste of everyone's time. With an NDA, all we're really saying is that neither side will talk about this to anyone else. Let's agree on that and move on.

Central Point of Contact

While this may seem elementary, many large companies miss this point. Not having a central point of contact for the startup to interact with can lead to days (or weeks) of emailing to find the right person for each specific deal term (for example: legal for certain terms, accounting for payment terms, and specific departments for other terms). Instead, having a single point person for directing traffic can speed things up significantly.

Including a central point of contact also helps you avoid what is known in psychology as the "Bystander Effect." We humans have an unfortunate tendency in groups to assume that someone else will do the job. A great example, which Robert Cialdini elaborates on in his classic book *Influence,* is if someone has a heart attack and is incapacitated in a crowded area, it's extremely likely for everyone to walk past the individual. We all tend to observe the behavior of those around us and use that to determine how we should act. In the case of the incapacitated individual, it's easy for us to see everyone walking past, think there must be nothing wrong with the person, and continue on with our day. What Cialdini recommends if you are ever in a situation where you're collapsing in a crowded area is to call out and point to a specific person while asking them to call 911. This allows you to circumvent the very human "Bystander Effect" flaw.

In other words, if everyone is in charge, then no one is in charge.

Looser Supply Chain Rules

With this recommendation, I might be giving nightmares to those who work in supply chain and quality assurance at large companies. But this is a really sticky point for startups trying to close enterprise deals. Understandably, supply chain and quality assurance departments are established in the first place to ensure that customers have a consistent experience, so changing this can be incredibly scary. That said, many large companies have supply-chain audits before working with new suppliers. The costs for this can run into six figures. While this might be fine for large companies, smaller companies may not (and likely don't) have the cash on hand to fund an audit like that, no matter how much revenue they might be getting once the deal closes. In the interest of expediting deals, large companies should look at how they can alter (or even remove) the supply-chain audit for deals below a certain size.

Budget Pre-approvals

In order to spend any money at a large company, there is a budget allocation, which needs to come from a decision-maker. The issue is not so much that these decision-makers need to be convinced—those decisions are often delegated to direct reports below a certain dollar value—but instead that they need to sign the paperwork. One way around this is to develop a pre-approval system for certain types of projects, which can be defined by dollar value, by category, or by some other variable. By having this pre-approval system in place, you can avoid delays that are simply due to paperwork getting signed.

Conclusion

Your company may have other procedures or ideas on how to fast-track startup deals. The most important thing is that this be given some thought. As we've seen, many so-called normal procedures within large companies are inadvertently but indisputably causing damage to startups. Improving these procedures and developing alternatives for startups can be a huge value add and become a point of differentiation between your company and your competitors.

CHAPTER 10

CONFERENCES, HACKATHONS, CONSULTANTS

Oh, My!

If you've spent any amount of time in the innovation world, you've probably seen the many different conferences, events, consulting firms, mastermind groups, university departments, and more that have popped up to champion that magic word: innovation. On one level, the rise of this ecosystem is somewhat predictable. As more companies admit to themselves that they need to do a better job of keeping up with the increased pace of innovation, there will of course be service providers who crop up to help them do exactly that. However, one would be challenged to find an industry where there are so many so-called experts with so little to show in the way of results. The endless service providers in the "innovation industry" might be an extreme case of the parasite phenomenon in all growing industries.

It's not too surprising that the innovation industry has attracted such a mass and variety of parasitical service providers.

The business of innovation is an admittedly risky one, though it certainly has lucrative rewards for those who succeed. Creating something new is a task that, even when done with perfect care and execution, has an astronomically high rate of failure. And for lack of a better way of stating this: the parasites hide in the failure rate. In other words, it's extremely difficult to distinguish between those who failed due to incompetence and those who failed because of timing, circumstances, or something else.

The reverse is also true. Take a look at the speaking circuit at innovation conferences, and you'll see that everyone has impressive credentials, whether that is as an early team member (or perhaps a founder) of a successful startup, investor, or intrapreneur. Perhaps this is obvious. After all, would a conference ever invite people to speak who didn't have a long list of credentials? But there's a bit of a fallacy here. Let's take a look.

Let's say a conference is advertising one of their speakers as an investor in successful startups like Facebook, Slack, and Uber. On the surface, that sounds great. What a strong roster! Not so fast! While those three companies are massive hits, it's important to know when this investor got involved. Being part of the seed round? Now that's impressive. Being part of the Series L round? Not so much. Obviously this is a simplistic example, but you can easily see why conference (or LinkedIn) headlines are a horrible way to judge expertise.

This could also be true for intrapreneurs or employees of famous startups. It's easy to be impressed by someone with Amazon on their résumé, but how do you know what role they truly had in the company's success? Successful companies have a "halo effect" on everyone affiliated with them, but the truth of the matter is that not everyone who works at a company has an instrumental role in the company's success. It might not be a nice thing to say, but companies usually have some A players, some B players, and plenty of C players. Someone who was instrumental to the company's strategy or developing/running a functional area deserves the halo effect. As harsh as it sounds, someone who was a mere cog in the wheel does not deserve this same halo effect.

The issue is not so much the mere existence of the C players, but the fact that the C players and the A players get lumped together by having been under the same roof. Going further, it's not uncommon to see a C player with a successful company on their résumé leverage that into more prominent roles or speaking gigs. But I'm not hating on the individuals who do this—as they say, "Don't hate the player, hate the game." So, I'm hating on the game.

This "skill by association" fallacy exists all over our society. Athlete, celebrity, and influencer product endorsements are the most common version of this, but it exists everywhere. In fact, startups use this strategy, too, when they use customer or press logos on their site (the "As Featured In" landing page section being Exhibit A).

The universal presence of this fallacy is evidence that the startup ecosystem isn't unique in using this form of—let's call it creative—marketing. That said, this strategy is leveraged by all parts of the startup corporate ecosystem, including conferences, consulting firms, and more. So when everyone is using this strategy, how does one sort the wheat from the chaff and figure out what's worth their time and what can be safely ignored? Let's dive in.

Startup Conferences

There is no shortage of startup conferences out there in the world. Every startup founder knows this. Especially with the rise of retargeting ads, sometimes it feels like you start getting pitched for attending or sponsoring startup conferences even before you officially start your company.

And before you get the wrong idea, I'm not hating on all startup conferences. A well-run and well-chosen event can be one of the highest ROI things you can do for your company. Especially in the early days, nothing beats face-to-face interaction, and a conference is a highly effective and cost-efficient way to do that. When I first started Unlimited Brewing Company, our first several customers were all people I met at events. I'm a true believer.

There are many different types of events out there. Sizes vary from a couple of dozen people to tens or even hundreds of thousands of people. Some are organized for a specific industry vertical, for example oil and gas, fashion, or beer. Others are organized by technology, such as artificial intelligence or machine learning. Others can be organized around specific audiences or types of consumers. And finally, others are created for specific purposes, such as connecting distributors and retailers, or even connecting startups and large companies. Attending or sponsoring the right type of event for your business can expand your lead list and take you to the next level in a matter of days. Furthermore, connecting with corporate decision-makers in person can "unblock" deals that have been stuck at some stage in the process for a while.

Arden Rosenblatt, founder & CEO of PieceMaker Technologies, on how his company uses events to grow the business:

In the early years, industry conferences were by far the best channel for us. In particular, Toy Fair NYC was one of our biggest events of the year. One of the reasons it was so important for us was Toy Fair enabled us to create a live experience, critical to selling the magic of custom-printed products on demand. Every year there was some form of custom giveaways 3D-printed on-site, from personalized NYC paraphernalia to 3D selfies. This experiential booth was quite purposeful: we had constant traffic throughout the show, and generated considerable buzz from strong press coverage and *Popular Science*'s "Best of Toy Fair 2016" Award.

Not only was this an opportunity to meet the major retailers and brands in the space, and to leave a strong impression, but it was also a great forum to check in with our partners and acquaintances, scheduling meetings right on-site to see how we can move forward.

Learn more about PieceMaker's work and interactions with large companies in the Appendix.

That said, choosing the wrong event can be a colossal waste of money. Sponsoring an event (or even just attending) can cost you tens of thousands, once you factor in tickets, airfare, hotel, food, swag with your company's name on it, and salaries. Startups especially can't afford to get their event strategy wrong. There isn't a whole lot of room for error, unless you are very well funded. So what should you look for when selecting which events to attend?

How to Choose the Right Event

This is one of those two-part equations: one side of the equation is what the event is offering, and the other side is what you need. If these aren't in equilibrium, the event likely will be a waste of money. The questions below will help guide you in selecting the right events to grow your company.

What Is Your Purpose?

Why exactly are you interested in attending or sponsoring a conference? Are you trying to raise awareness of what you're doing? Are you trying to meet potential customers? Are you looking to build and maintain relationships with industry veterans and influencers? Are you looking to recruit?

These are all legitimate reasons to attend an event. The key is being honest with yourself and understanding what is driving you to certain events. Just the fact that your peers or competitors will be there is a terrible reason for attending. Once you know your purpose, you can narrow your scope to the events that fit your purpose, rather than looking at the whole wide world of events.

Some events, particularly hackathons, are geared primarily at recruiting. Others can be specifically geared toward making connections between small brands and distributors. Purposes vary widely, so having a blanket event strategy is generally not a great idea.

How Do You Know Who Is Attending?

Assuming you're looking to connect with your corporate counterparts at specific companies, it can be difficult to know just who is attending. Many event companies will put a bunch of logos on their website of companies attending the event. But as we saw earlier, due to the nature of corporate silos, finding the *right* person is the key, not just anyone within the specific company.

One way to determine the types of individuals attending the event is to look at the speaker list of the event. Most events publicize their speakers on their website. This page usually includes names, job titles, and sometimes even links to their social media profiles (such as LinkedIn). This should give you a good sense of the audience. For example, if you're looking to connect with Under Armour's marketing department at an event that Under Armour is listed as attending, but you look at the speaker list and only see Research & Development speakers, it probably isn't the right event for you.

Another tactic I've seen some startups use, especially for events they are considering sponsoring, is to ask the sponsorship director (or whoever is trying to sell to them) about the attendee list. The event sponsorship director is in the business of selling, and therefore doing whatever he or she can do to close the deal. They are more likely than anyone else to find and share the information you're looking for. This doesn't always work—but, as they say, it doesn't cost you anything to ask.

I asked Brian Ardinger, host of the Inside/Outside Innovation podcast and the founder of the Inside/Outside Innovation Summit, about the origins of his event, why it's valuable to startups, and finally what he does to ensure that relevant connections are made at the event:

The [Inside/Outside Innovation] podcast's original inspiration was to look at tech startups outside the Valley. Then it morphed into talking to innovators inside and outside of large companies. The conference came by us noticing that there's a real need to bring people from the two different backgrounds—startup and

(continued on next page)

(continued from previous page)

corporate—into the same room. We wanted to see what would happen when you bring the "ties and the T-shirts" together.

Part of our goal with the conference is to scare the pants off corporate and show them the scale of innovation taking place. The days of a business model lasting fifty years are gone. So we try to give companies the context of innovation and exposure to startups who are building new things. It provides perspective. Seeing a two-person team being able to spin something up gives you a different outlook and shows you what's really possible.

We try to find corporate innovators that are already attempting to be more innovative—for example, people who are trying to use lean startup methodology or innovators running their own accelerator or lab. This ensures that the connections are relevant for everyone involved.

To read Brian's full interview and learn more about his work, please see the Appendix.

What Types of Events Should Be Avoided?

I am personally not a fan of conferences based on "innovation." There are exceptions (the Inside/Outside Innovation Summit comes to mind); but in general, innovation conferences get a lot of thinkers/academic types and not a lot of doers. Even if these types of conferences have attendees who work at the companies you are trying to sell to, you're more likely to connect with individuals who don't have the ability to move a deal forward. This, of course, is not always true, but a heuristic to use to save yourself money, time, and pain.

Following Up After an Event

The purpose of attending an event isn't just to collect business cards. Your goal is to take all these new connections and turn them into business. This starts at the event itself and then continues through to the follow-up after the event.

When you meet someone at an event, your conversation will generally reach a point where you figure out something you'd like to follow up on, at which point you'll likely exchange cards. The problem is that you can meet so many people at an event that you end up with a jumble of business cards and no idea which conversations you need to follow up on and which ones are just pleasantries.

To solve this, I recommend developing some type of system to track follow-ups. This could be as simple as a note in your phone or even just marking business cards with a checkmark or some other symbol to indicate that you need to follow up.

Consultants

Once you spend some time in the corporate innovation space, you'll begin to see the sheer number of consultants in the industry. The prevalence of consultants in this space can be mind-boggling and difficult to sort out. How do you know who is worth working with and who isn't?

In my experience, it can be worth working with consultants who can deliver a tangible benefit that doesn't require them to have a long-term commitment to your company. For example, if you're trying to enter a new vertical with your product, particularly one in which you and your team have little experience, it can be worth hiring a consultant from that vertical. This use case is particularly well suited to consultants because the results are easily measurable and can deliver a tangible benefit that would take you considerably longer to achieve on your own. The same could be true for a product consultant who is redesigning one of your features. On the other hand, I would *not* recommend a consultant for anything strategy-related. This has the potential to become an infinite project, with no beginning or end, and—even worse—with no tangible results.

If you plan to work with any consultants, I highly recommend structuring a deal that aligns their incentives with your startup. If you're bringing them on to help you close deals, it can be structured so most of their compensation comes from closing deals. If you're bringing them on to build something, their payment can be based on successfully completing the project. The key is to make sure you don't have a perverse incentive structure that is detrimental to your long-term success.

The most common detrimental compensation structure is to pay consultants hourly. This is not just an unaligned structure; it is a structure in which the consultant's incentive is the exact opposite of yours! Look carefully: you hire a consultant to complete a task. That means you want the task completed successfully as soon as possible. However, in this structure, it is in the consultant's interest to take *as long as possible* instead of finishing as quickly as possible. This doesn't happen all the time, but it certainly increases the odds that you'll pay more than you need to. Avoid the hourly compensation structure if possible.

That said, consultants can add massive value in the right circumstances. Justin Mares, founder and CEO of Kettle & Fire, a revolutionary all-natural bone-broth brand, was able to get their product distributed into all Whole Foods stores by working with a network of retail brokers. This is a great example of the power of working with outside consultants. The right individuals can move your business forward without increasing your team or being a permanent addition to your team. They can come in, get the job done, and leave.

Bill Belias has worked with startups and large companies for years as a consultant, adviser, inventor, and strategist. He specializes in developing novel packaging technologies. I asked him about what the best-case argument would be for bringing in a consultant:

The interesting thing is that consultants are often thought of as experts, but I don't think that's necessarily the main reason that would make a consultant effective. I believe that a consultant has the ability to focus on a problem without the noise that's found in a company. A company usually has a number of— let's say fifty—people who are all involved in a given project. And they're never involved full-time, they're just in and out. Whereas a consultant who is brought in to work on a problem looks at it differently. They are able to focus. It's like bringing in a computer that's brought in to focus on one algorithm, as opposed to a server that's working on many different programs at once.

Within companies, there's this sense that when they bring in a consultant, that person needs to be an expert. Little do they realize that learning to be an expert is a skill. And that skill happens to be something that consultants are often good at.

Consultants also have less fear—which is important for innovation. There are many types of fear, such as "my boss is going to think I'm stupid" or "if I make a mistake, I'll get fired." With

(continued on next page)

(continued from previous page)

employees, people often prioritize their promotions over the task at hand. Whereas a consultant knows that there is never a promotion coming to them, so they are much more focused on the task at hand.

To learn more about Bill's thoughts on the startup-corporate ecosystem, please read his full interview in the Appendix.

Of course, it isn't always possible to pay consultants purely based on performance. Sales are easily quantifiable; but what about design? Or product development? For these types of consultants, some type of project-based compensation is usually best. Exact payment structures vary by project, but 50 percent payment up front and 50 percent on completion is commonly used. A good heuristic to use when considering a consultant is whether or not they are willing to have at least part of their compensation tied to performance. If they aren't, there's a good chance that they are of the "leech" variety. If the consultant is at least willing to consider performance-based compensation, give them a further look. Skin in the game is the ultimate filter.

Conclusion

The noise surrounding the startup-corporate ecosystem can be extremely tough to sort out. By having a strong filter and looking at incentives, you'll be better able to decipher who is worth your time and who is just after your money. Choose wisely.

CHAPTER 11

EMPATHY

The Final Ingredient to Productive Startup-Corporate Interactions

Given the differences in incentives, structure, and culture that have been presented in this book, you would be forgiven for thinking there was an insurmountable barrier between startups and large corporations that would keep them from ever developing a mutual understanding. While it's true that there are difficulties in these distinct types of organizations working together, this difference is by no means insurmountable. However, there's only one way I've ever come across that enables one to cross this divide (no matter which side you're crossing from). That method is empathy.

Empathy is a strange thing. Empathy allows us to put ourselves in the shoes of others, to experience what they experience. By identifying ourselves with the experience of the other (who is, admittedly, sometimes our adversary), we are able to understand the "why" of their actions, instead of viewing their actions as deliberate attempts to frustrate us.

Having sat on both sides of the startup and corporate eco-system, I perhaps have an unfair advantage in understanding the motives, challenges, and incentives of each side. Often, I hear people on either side question the motives and competence of their counterparts. Startup founders often think that only those without creativity and with a desire for bureaucracy go into the corporate world. Those who work in large corporations some-times think that entrepreneurs are all swashbuckling risk-takers without any regard for process, organization, or prudence. And, of course, the longer one is entrenched on their particular side of the debate, the more convinced they are that their side is always right and that the other side is always wrong. Compound this with the fact that entrepreneurs tend to be friends mostly with other startup folks and corporate employees are friends with other corporate employees, and you have a ready-made echo-chamber problem.

Here's the truth of the matter: both sides are simply trying their best. They are doing their best with the tools and incen-tives at their disposal. This should be highly comforting to both startup and corporate folks. This means there is no malicious intent when things don't go well. There is no deliberate sabotage of deals. In fact, the opposite is true—both sides are trying their absolute damn best to get productive deals done.

And yet, if that's true, then how come so many of these seem-ingly mutually beneficial deals can't get across the finish line? What's holding everyone back?

My take on this situation is that there is currently a major lack of empathy between startups and large corporations. And this lack of empathy is to blame for the current pathetic state of affairs. And yet there is good news. Empathy is the key to bridging the gap between startups and corporates. This is what this chapter is focused on.

Why Empathy?

You may be sitting there thinking that empathy is an awfully soft thing to point to as the magic tool to bridge the startup-corporate divide. But empathy is, in fact, one of the key cognitive abilities that makes us human.

We humans have a unique ability to mentally imagine ourselves in situations that we are not actually in. While this can sometimes be a curse (anyone who has ever found themselves imagining worst-case scenarios can attest to this), in this instance it's a blessing. This ability to imagine what isn't actually present allows us to plan ahead in order to solve future problems, examine the past to learn from prior mistakes, and defer rewards in the present for a greater reward in the future.

Empathy takes this imagining a step further. It allows us to actually "feel" what another individual is experiencing, to identify with those emotions at a level where you are actually feeling the other person's joy, pain, excitement, or another emotion right along with them. In a phrase, this is "putting yourself in someone else's shoes."

Empathy, then, is one of our core strengths and differentiators as human beings. It has the power to resolve conflicts both big and small. And this includes bridging the divide between large companies and startups.

Brian Ardinger, an innovator who has sat on many sides of the startup-corporate table, gave this advice when I asked him what he wished startups knew about large companies and vice versa:
(continued on next page)

(continued from previous page)

I've noticed that the startups that are good at working with cor-porates tend to be ones with founders who have worked on the corporate side. Sometimes startups can get cocky about disrupting the industry, etc., etc. Don't get cocky about things, and really work to find your advocate within your target corpo-rate partner.

I also always wish corporates understood how fast and fu-rious the startup side is and how any delay can really have a big effect on a startup. I wish they would recognize that any time you engage with a startup, you are taking them off their game. Understand that taking two or three weeks to schedule a meeting is normal pace on the corporate side but is a huge deal on the startup side. Respecting the speed at which a startup has to move to basically maintain its life is oftentimes overlooked, especially if the corporate person has never been in a startup.

You can read more about Brian's thoughts on the startup-corporate ecosystem in the Appendix.

How Startups Can Empathize with Their Corporate Counterparts

If you're on the startup side of the table, you're probably asking yourself why in the world I'm calling out startups first for their lack of empathy with their corporate counterparts. Isn't it common knowledge that corporates are the real ones struggling to understand the other side?

While it is true that corporate innovators struggle to put themselves in the shoes of their startup partners, that doesn't get startups off the hook. The truth of the matter is that startups have just as much difficulty in understanding the world of corporate innovators. That said, there are a few concrete steps startup folks can take to better understand their corporate counterparts.

Don't Patronize—The Other Side Isn't Dumb

One of the biggest problems on the startup side of the startup-corporate intersection is a widely held assumption that people who are in corporate, particularly those who have been in corporate for a long time, are in some way intellectually inferior to those in the startup world. This assumption couldn't be further from the truth. No, your corporate counterpart probably doesn't use HackerNews, reddit, or Product Hunt as much as you do (though that's not always true); but the use of those startup platforms has nothing to do with intelligence. The use of those platforms is simply a reflection of being in the startup echo chamber. Nothing more.

One thing I hear often (and said in my pre-corporate days) is the sentiment that "if the person in corporate were smarter or more driven, they would be creating something rather than collecting a paycheck." But this sentiment is purely an assumption. There are an infinite number of reasons that could have driven someone into corporate. We don't have any right to make assumptions about someone's background, goals, intelligence, and motivations simply by virtue of their having a corporate job at the exact moment in time that we start interacting with their employer.

Something that goes hand in hand with this "corporate people are dumb" assumption is the patronization that can occur when startups pitch corporate partners. I've sat in on meetings when startup teams lectured some of the largest and best-regarded brands in the world on the concept of branding. Don't be like them. Good startup sales- and business-development people treat their potential corporate partners with the respect they deserve. And the best keep their eyes and ears open, too—after all, the large companies have definitely figured *something* out successfully in order to get to their current size.

Avoid Startup Jargon

The flip side to assuming the other side is dumb is to assume that they know and use all the same startup jargon as you do. I made this mistake myself many times, even after I joined corporate. Earlier, I mentioned how a senior leader of a corporate R&D lab I worked with thought the "accelerators" I was referring to were particle accelerators. But I've made equally bad mistakes, like assuming everyone subscribes to Product Hunt, follows venture capital trends, and generally stays within the startup echo chamber.

I've found using acronyms and initialisms to be one of the worst mistakes to make when trying to work with a corporate counterpart. Terms like LTV, CAC, and CTR are not real things outside of the startup/tech world, besides in some corporate marketing departments. You certainly won't find people in the finance department using terms like this. Just spell these things out, at least the first few times you use them, so you can be sure that everyone knows what you're referring to.

In short, speak the language of your potential partner, and save the startup jargon for your team and your startup buddies.

Get to the Decision-Maker

Back in my corporate days, I was in what I like to refer to as a position of influence, rather than a position of power. This meant that while I could introduce startups to key decision-makers within the company and hopefully influence their decisions with my recommendations, I had no decision-making authority of my own. Having sat on the startup side of the table before, I tried to make this as clear to startups as possible, usually bringing it up right at the start of the introductory meeting. Even with that disclaimer, there were more instances than I can count where a startup salesperson or founder would try to push me into making a decision.

The only thing you can accomplish by trying to push a non-decision-maker into making a decision is that you will annoy them out of ever wanting to use whatever influence they have to help you. The better way to deal with this is to quickly find out who the decision-maker is and then see if you can get introduced to that individual (or team) through the contacts you currently have.

Sometimes this process can become a bit convoluted. Large companies have so many departments and employees that it isn't always clear who has responsibility for which functions. Adding to the confusion, startups often operate at the intersection of multiple fields or in an entirely new field altogether, and therefore do not fit neatly into any of the preset corporate departments and hierarchies. Don't worry about this: if you have a valuable offering, you can always find someone internally who has both the budget and the desire to add your technology to their fiefdom. Finding this person can be tricky (it sometimes feels a bit like trying to solve a puzzle . . .) but it's certainly doable. Above all, don't try to pressure someone with no authority to make a decision. That will get you nowhere and ultimately just rub people the wrong way.

Make Life Easy for Your Corporate Counterpart

This one might sound overly obvious, but it is shocking how few companies actually do this. As we've discussed, once you've convinced your corporate counterpart of the value of your product, service, idea, whatever—the next step is that they need to sell it internally to their team and superiors. But this is where things start going off the rails. Tell me if the following process sounds familiar:

Step 1: Great initial conversation with your counterpart, who says she needs to speak with her team and will get back to you ASAP with next steps. You mentally start celebrating the massive sale you're about to make.

Step 2: *crickets chirping*

Step 3: You follow up. Many times.

Step 4: Months later, you get an email saying that "after much internal discussion, we've decided not to move forward at this time."

These steps are the bane of every salesperson's existence. And while there are many reasons why these events could have transpired (sales is an art, not a science, after all), the most common one I've seen is not understanding what takes place after your initial pitch.

After you have some interest from your corporate counterpart, the next step on their end is going to be convincing their team of the merits of your solution. This is surprisingly true, even if you're working with the "decision-maker." Many companies, but large companies in particular, tend to make decisions by consensus, and this can cause huge problems for you in the sales process. The biggest reason? You're now asking someone to pitch the merits and value of your solution who has spent all of thirty minutes learning about it. Their team is going to poke holes in the idea, and your counterpart will not know how to respond. Instead, they'll start thinking that perhaps they got overexcited during your pitch or that their team knows more than they do in your particular field.

Dave Knox, author of Predicting the Turn, *co-founder of The Brandery startup accelerator in Cincinnati, and CMO of Rockfish (acquired by WPP), had this advice for startups who are looking to work with large companies:*

You as a startup are going to move incredibly fast, because you have a burn rate. Your conversation with your corporate counterpart is probably your most important conversation of the day. Conversely, for the person in corporate, their conversation with you is highly unlikely to be their most important conversation of the day.

You as a startup founder can typically make decisions as you want. Meanwhile, in the large company there are checks and balances that require buy-in from multiple stakeholders. So that means your internal champion is probably fighting hard on your behalf, but that there is a process for them to go through that may require approval from four, five, or six different people. Being cognizant of that and doing what you can to make your champion's life easier can be powerful. But you need to be patient.

To read Dave's complete interview, please visit the Appendix.

This is where the best startups differentiate themselves. The best startups create materials that they can arm their corporate champions with to better sell the value internally. This could include samples (for physical-product businesses), well-designed decks, video demos, testimonials, customer referrals, and much more. For certain accounts, you may even offer to travel to the company and meet with their team in person. In fact, this is ideal, though it can be cost-prohibitive depending on the stage of your company. But even in this day and age of digital-first, there is nothing that works better than an in-person pitch, especially in the corporate world.

Along those same lines, even once you have an initial deal (or, more commonly, a pilot), your job doesn't change. Namely, you need to help your corporate counterpart look smart for deciding to work with you. There are many ways to do this, but one of the best methods I've seen is to issue regular reports with results on the value of your program. The specifics depend on your product, of course, but any metrics that matter to your counterpart will be relevant here: impressions, clicks, revenue, new customers, press generated. Put in a more general way, anything you can provide your corporate counterpart with that will make them look good to their boss is valuable to you. Remember, looking good to their superiors is the main reason they're working with you in the first place.

Be Useful Beyond the Deal

Let me describe two different salespeople. Salesperson #1 is friendly, easy to get along with, isn't pushy, talks business when necessary but not exclusively, and always has fun stories and interesting news to share. Salesperson #2 is all business. They only see sales targets as prospects, not human beings. No small talk or making friends for Salesperson #2. Who would you rather do business with?

It isn't rocket science: even if we try to be objective about different products and solutions, we like doing business with people we like and who are useful to us. As Robert Cialdini explained in *Influence*, there are a few factors that power the "Liking Principle":

1. *Physical Attractiveness*—we associate good looks with other favorable traits
2. *Similarity*—we like people similar to us
3. *Compliments*—we like people who praise us
4. *Contact and Cooperation*—we like it when we work with others who have the same goals as we do
5. *Conditioning and Association*—we associate people or things we like with the other things they are associated with (for example: an attractive model next to a car)

There's not much you can do about Physical Attractiveness (besides making sure you don't look like a slob), but the other four principles are all important in becoming a great salesperson. The unifying principle here is that finding commonality is the key. And finding commonality is rooted in empathy.

Being likeable and being useful go hand in hand. The best salespeople I've ever seen are the ones who find ways to be useful and helpful to their potential clients *whether or not they ever end up buying anything from them*. That last part is crucial. The average salesperson finds ways to be useful while a deal is ongoing, but the best ones are useful and helpful all the time.

This all goes back to making your corporate counterpart's life easier and better. If you find an article that would be relevant to your counterpart, share it with them. If you come across another startup that looks interesting or could solve a problem your counterpart mentioned, send it to them. If you have an introduction or speaking opportunity that could help your counterpart's career, by all means make the introduction. And be genuine about it. There's nothing worse than a salesperson who comes across as disingenuous. You would think the idea of being useful beyond just the deal you're working on would be obvious; but judging by the behavior of most salespeople out there, the lesson hasn't quite sunk in yet.

Have a desire to help people, and good things will happen. It's almost as if the people who came up with the concept of karma knew something.

Work Within the Process

This is one of those "last but not least" types of tips. It goes without saying that many corporate processes can be . . . convoluted, to say the least. Most of the time, the corporate side of the equation turns into a black hole, especially the legal and finance departments. This can lead to a lot of frustration for startups and cause them to search for ways around the system. This is understandable but, ultimately, not something that I advise.

Being resourceful is a desirable trait for startup founders and salespeople. But there is such a thing as trying to get too creative and hurting yourself along the way. While the decision-maker who ultimately gives the go-ahead on working with your startup is technically the "decision-maker," your deal can still get derailed by one of the various legal and contract negotiation groups (sometimes called supplier relations or procurement) that large companies have.

Chaz Giles, formerly of Citi Ventures, P&G, and MomTrusted. com and currently Global Head of External Innovation at The Estée Lauder Companies, advised that startups try to understand how to work within large companies in the following manner:

The biggest thing is that literally everything is different. The time horizons are different, the metrics are different, the priorities are different. It's all different.

This means you need to understand all of this and plan for it. That could mean a different sales strategy or even a different fund-raising strategy. You could do things like partner with an existing vendor so you can avoid the procurement process, etc.

But most importantly, you need to study how large companies interact and operate.

Some companies are worse with this than others, but all large companies will make you jump through some hoops to get a contract through. We've talked elsewhere about how to deal with these groups, but the key thing to remember is that the people you're interacting with don't make the rules: they're just following the rules that the corporation has created for them. As frustrating as that can be (and trust me, it can be pretty frustrating), be empathetic to the people in these groups, do what you can to make their lives easier, and ultimately work within the process.

Something that will make you less frustrated: plan for the contract negotiation and legal approval time line when you forecast how long your deals will take to close.

How Corporate Innovators Can Empathize with Their Startup Counterparts

For someone who has never worked for or founded a startup, it can be really tough to imagine the struggles, stress, and risk that founders experience on a daily basis. Building something from scratch, especially with limited resources, is really, really difficult, and founders in particular (but all startup employees) have to live with the uncertainty and emotional roller coaster.

One example that does a great job of shining light on the differences in perception of uncertainty between startups and corporations is layoffs. A startup salesperson (or any employee) knows that if performance drops, either by them or by the company as a whole, there is an extremely high likelihood (if not the certainty) of layoffs. It's just part of the startup game. In corporate, even the threat of layoffs creates an (understandably) extremely worrying situation. This is just one example of the uncertainty that startup founders and employees live with every day.

Knowing and understanding the stresses that startups face can help get better deals more quickly, and with better terms for everyone. Here are a few specific areas for corporate innovators to focus on:

Be Honest and Up Front about Your Interest

This is a good rule in general, whether it's for dating or for startup-corporate interactions: be honest about your intentions. Specifically for startup-corporate interactions, if you're speaking with a startup, don't pretend like you're interested in buying their product or service if you're not actually interested in doing so. Similarly, if you have no decision-making authority, it's not a good idea to pretend that you have it.

"Life is a game of inches" is a quote that applies as well to startups as it does to sports. In startups, seemingly little decisions—like which clients to focus on—can literally make or break the company. And for precisely that reason, when corporate innovators (or wannabes) act interested when they aren't, indicate buying authority when they have none, or in general act in ways that obscure their true intentions, this can have drastic unintended consequences.

The best way to make sure you're honest and up front is to be extremely clear during the first conversation with your startup counterpart on exactly what you're responsible for and why you're interested in talking.

Honesty is the best policy.

Don't Get Their Hopes Up

This is very much related to being honest. What you, the corporate person, say has ramifications beyond what you intend. When you tell a startup that you see a "very good chance of moving forward," the startup is going to make decisions in hiring, fund-raising, and product road map that are trade-offs against other things they could invest in.

The solution for this is to always skew conservative (in the nonpolitical sense) and/or pessimistic when you discuss time lines and odds of getting a deal done, especially when interacting with your startup counterpart. If you think it's likely that it will take three months to close a deal, estimate six months. Trust me, your startup counterpart will not begrudge you for getting the deal done sooner than expected.

On a related note, I also advise being very clear on the steps involved to close a deal: whose buy-in is necessary, the contract hurdles that need to be cleared, any budget constraints, and any nonnegotiable contract terms. These go a very long way toward keeping everyone's expectations aligned so there are no resentments later on.

Be Conscientious about Deal Closing Times

Something I've alluded to throughout this book is the value to startups of time. Most startups are not profitable, especially early on. There is a certain amount of money in the bank, most of which is either brought in from investors or is self-funded by the founders; and every day, there is less money in the bank. Logically, that means most startups have an "expiration date"—the day they will run out of money. This is (obviously) extremely stressful for everyone involved in the company: founders, employees, and even investors.

Chaz Giles, formerly of Citi Ventures, P&G, and MomTrusted. com and currently Global Head of External Innovation at The Estée Lauder Companies, has some advice for how corporate innovators can make the lives of their startup counterparts easier:

Corporate innovators need to understand the speed at which startups move and, because of that, the need for clarity. If you respect those things and are clear and transparent with what you can and can't do, you'll have some great interactions. Similarly, make sure you follow up. Too many times there are great meetings that large companies have with small ones, but then priorities change and things happen without any follow-up. I really think this is where reputations are won—and lost—for large companies among startups.

For example, by being clear and precise on why you aren't moving forward, the startup can incorporate that feedback and iterate, so that in four to six months, when they come back, now they've helped you solve your problem and you're eager to engage with them. But that iteration can only happen if you are clear and brutally honest with feedback.

In addition, I think large organizations need to have translators (people who have been on both sides of the ecosystem) who can help to cut through the language, so to speak. Oftentimes, there's an unmet need in translating between what large companies are saying and what startups are saying.

Finally, large companies should consider putting together an "innovation execution" function. As I said earlier, on paper an innovation opportunity might make sense; but to actually go execute, today that falls to the business units, who are often already running at full capacity. So having other teams and groups who can implement pilots, build new functions, and create connections between brand and technology. This would change conversations with business units from a hypothetical business impact to "this technology led to an X% lift in revenue during the pilot." Things become much more tangible, and it is easier to know how to prioritize and invest.

To read Chaz's complete interview, please visit the Appendix.

One of the most helpful things you can do when working with startups as a corporate innovator is doing things to speed up deal-closing times. If this means you need to start the supplier-review process before exact deal terms are negotiated, then you should do that. If it means having the startup speak with legal before you've fully committed to working with them, so be it.

Anything you can do to speed up closing the deal is incredibly valuable to your startup partners.

Be Observant of Legal Costs

Day-to-day legal costs are something that large companies (with their armies of corporate lawyers) don't really think much about. But for startups, who are often paying their lawyers by the hour on an as-needed basis, every interaction with a lawyer costs them more of their already-limited cash. And as we all know, lawyers aren't cheap.

One thing to strongly avoid is having startups engage in an endless back-and-forth with your legal team. This can cost your counterparts a small fortune and leads to resentment before the relationship even begins. Instead, have your lawyers make their concerns clear in the beginning and only negotiate the most crucial points.

A program that works extremely well, which more companies are starting to offer, is a type of "fast track" for startups they work with. This type of program involves more straightforward contracts, more clear payment terms, and, most importantly, extremely legal back-and-forth. I highly recommend considering if a program like this would be useful for your company.

Pay On Time . . . and Offer Helpful Payment Terms

This seems obvious; but unfortunately for many companies, it isn't. Large companies are blessed with being profitable (most of them, anyway) and are often sitting on cash. Meanwhile, startups are often bleeding cash and desperately need the revenue to help them continue to make payroll.

Despite this state of affairs, it's quite common for large companies to pay their startup counterparts late and/or make them jump through hoops to get paid. And honestly, what can the startup do about it? If a giant customer pays them late, they obviously aren't going to sue them. This comes down to ignorance—on the part of many large companies—of the immense importance of cash for their startup counterparts.

Being helpful on payment terms can also be a smart business decision, not just an ethical one. Back in my corporate days, something we occasionally utilized was providing favorable payment terms to a startup (for example, full payment up front instead of monthly) in exchange for some other deal term that we wanted, such as a lower price or industry exclusivity. Sometimes life presents such a commonsense solution that it's shocking it isn't widely utilized.

Conclusion

My hope is that by shedding some light on the struggles of both the corporate and startup innovators of the world, we'll be able to create a better ecosystem for all. There are so many deals and partnerships that *should* happen but don't, often because of tactical failures by either or both sides. It's time this ends. Mutual understanding and empathy are the keys to unlocking the massive potential deals between startups and large companies.

ACKNOWLEDGMENTS

Where do I even begin this? First of all, a big thank-you to *you*, the reader. There would be no book without you and your curiosity about this topic. Hopefully the book achieved what it set out to do, namely pulling back the curtain on the structure and motivations of those who work at large companies and how you can use that information to better work with these organizations.

A huge thank-you goes out to Chaz Giles, who has put up with me since my days working for him at Mom Trusted and brought me into Estée Lauder despite my lack of experience with large companies. He has exceeded every expectation I could ever have had for a mentor. It feels weird to refer to him as a mentor—a better word would be "brother."

Thank you to all the wonderful folks I worked with at The Estée Lauder Companies. The warmth, love, and sense of family I felt from everyone I came in contact with was something I didn't know was possible in a massive company. I will be forever grateful for the patience everyone showed me as a rookie, both in cosmetics and in large organizations.

Thank you to everyone who took the time to speak with me about this book and helped build and clarify these ideas. Dave Knox, Dave Lishego, Sean Ammirati, Bill Belias, Arden Rosenblatt, Nim De Swardt, Justin Mares, Brian Ardinger, and Sebastian Metti immediately come to mind, but the ideas in this book have been crafted over hundreds of conversations with countless others.

Thank you to my agent, Laurie Abkemeier, who believed in my abilities and my very raw original book proposal from the beginning and was incredibly patient as this book came together. Thank you to my editor, Tim Burgard. This book literally wouldn't exist without you.

Thank you to my brother, Jay, for always being a patient sounding board for me, even when my ideas are silly or I'm just ranting about things. Or quoting *The Office*.

And last but most important, thank you to my parents for originally suggesting that I start taking notes on what I was observing in the corporate world, because it could be useful to others. And of course, thank you for always having my back no matter what. I wouldn't be anything without you and your sacrifices.

APPENDIX 1

FULL INTERVIEW TRANSCRIPTS

I'm beyond grateful for the wonderful people who gave me so much of their time to help turn this book into a reality. Some of these interviews were so deep and insightful that it seemed like a waste not to include them in their entirety. Here they are:

Interview with Arden Rosenblatt, Founder and CEO of PieceMaker Technologies

Tell me about your experience as a founder working with large companies.

PieceMaker has been fortunate to work with a variety of large companies. The first major company we worked with was Toys"R"Us, where we piloted several in-store 3D printing kiosks in New York, New Jersey, and Pennsylvania. We first met the team from Toys"R"Us at Toy Fair NYC, the country's largest toy-industry expo held at the Javits Center each year. For PieceMaker, it's the big event of the year and where we made a lot of strong early connections. By the end of 2014, we were gearing up to pilot the earliest prototype of 3D printing kiosks for mass retail.

Overall, it was a great experience and introduction to navigating corporate for us. Toys"R"Us was enthusiastic to bring these experiences to life, but we had to meet the same hurdles that any children's product would need to, both from a safety/reliability/operations perspective, and also in terms of sales. While this brought some challenges to a young company working with a large partner for the first time, it ended up making us much stronger. All our printers and equipment became certified to UL spec, our printable content was tested to meet US child safety standards for ages 3+ (making us first in the country), and the design of our kiosk benefited greatly from Toys"R"Us's expertise in installation, retail operations, and customer experiences.

While there can be many aspects of working with large companies that are frustrating to small companies and startups, like the sluggish pace, in the best-case scenario large partners can provide invaluable knowledge and mentorship. For early-stage companies, the associated guidance and expertise may be one of the most valuable aspects of the deal. We carried this philosophy to our work with Ford Motors and Nickelodeon, bringing their branded content to life as customizable, 3D printable toys, accessories, and souvenirs. Now that we had the important stuff out of the way (security, reliability, safety, etc.), these incredible brands help us fine-tune our product design, helping us learn across product lines how to make toys kids love.

Since expanding outside the toy industry, PieceMaker has done more direct B2B work in a variety of markets; however, that magic formula doesn't change. We believe strongly that combining the laser focus and street experience that startups bring with the scale and expertise of large companies is the formula for success in innovation. When either party goes it alone, they are inevitably forced outside their comfort zone, where it's easy to make very costly mistakes.

PieceMaker has also worked with ExOne (Metal 3D Printing), Paul Michael Design (Jewelry), and other companies in a variety of industries.

Any major successes you'd like to elaborate on?

I think we've had a fair share of major breakthroughs made possible through our work with corporate partners. Much of the work PieceMaker did with venues like Toys"R"Us or the Indianapolis Children's Museum was groundbreaking. These were the first retail 3D printing systems, the first printed line of children's toys approved for sale in the US, the first customizable printed product lines for partners like Nickelodeon or Ford, the first AM systems to be operated by non-technical retail staff, and the list goes on.

On a personal level, one of our biggest successes was enabling anyone (mostly ages 5+) to create meaningfully customized, one-of-a-kind 3D products for the first time. The look on each customer's face when they received the piece they had just designed was always the same, across thousands of families. It's the same look we had when we started 3D printing, one where you can see the universe expanding in a person's mind. We believe very strongly in the democratizing power of digital manufacturing, so it's very rewarding to see that reinforced time and time again with normal families from across the country and globe.

Just as important, are there any failures you'd like to point to?

I think many would view the fact that we are not currently operating retail printing kiosks as a failure. To some degree, I would agree; but overall I don't view this as a failure. Our intention from the beginning was to test the best ways to bring a radically new product and channel to market. On a store level, the results were incredibly promising, with sales reaching up to $1,000 per day from a single station (using about $15 of raw material). However, scaling the deployment, operation, and maintenance of hundreds or thousands of kiosks is a very different undertaking, one that requires VC support. Raising VC money was an area I couldn't make it happen, and we had to shift business plans.

That being said, overall we consider each one of these relationships incredibly positive. As mentioned above, they helped us develop unique expertise on AM systems and supply chains that has enabled us to join the B2B market in a serious way. They helped us develop end-to-end systems that are safe, secure, efficient, and profitable. Without this history, we wouldn't be able to work the exciting projects we do today that continue to push the boundaries of digital manufacturing. It may not be a road map to world domination, as retail kiosks might have been, but we're continuing to grow revenue and bring our technology to some of the best brands in the world to create next-generation experiences, products, and supply chains.

When approaching a large company, what does your process look like?

We usually try to connect on a personal level, whether through word of mouth, introductions through our network, or at industry conferences. In our experience, these are the most successful relationships.

In the early years, industry conferences were by far the best channel for us. In particular, Toy Fair NYC was one of our biggest events of the year. One of the reasons it was so important for us was Toy Fair enabled us to create a live experience, critical to selling the magic of custom-printed products on demand. Every year, there was some form of custom giveaways 3D-printed on-site, from personalized NYC paraphernalia to 3D selfies. This experiential booth was quite purposeful: we had constant traffic throughout the show, and it generated considerable buzz from strong press coverage and *Popular Science*'s "Best of Toy Fair 2016" Award.

Not only was this an opportunity to meet the major retailers and brands in the space, and to leave a strong impression, but it was also a great forum to check in with our partners and acquaintances, scheduling meetings right on-site to see how we can move forward.

Have you ever made a mistake when approaching or trying to close a deal with a large company?

In general . . . it's hard to say, but I don't think so. We've definitely blown it with investors. Once, I had a deal in the works with an investor who was very excited, and would have been an exceptional asset. I decided to bring some additional members of my team in to listen, but it fell apart pretty quickly. They started asking a lot of questions and for feedback on our business. I lost control of the meeting, and essentially the deal fell apart from there. I've also had an investment fall through because they didn't like an answer I gave after a pitch.

The corporate world is very different than investment . . . much less mercurial. I think it goes back to my earlier answers—those that don't really need your solution will find any excuse to get spooked. Those that genuinely need what you do, and have a clear sense of where it fits into their road map . . . they are the ones who will push a deal through.

With that in mind, I'm sure we've made a few teams nervous when we get overly aggressive on getting contracts signed and payments on a regular schedule—cash is king at a startup—however, it has never been to the point of killing a deal or relationship. More the normal back-and-forth between a hungry small company and large organizations dealing with bureaucracy and looking to use their leverage to get the best deal and longest deferments of payment possible.

When there is shared understanding and passion on both sides, most deals seem >90% likely to close. The rare exception is when an entire project gets killed from the higher-ups.

Who do you typically approach within a large company?

Because we are working with consumer-facing technology, we often connect first with innovation teams. From there, marketing and engineering often come in to tweak the specs to meet their needs.

How do you navigate through the maze of departments and employees within large companies?

We've found that it's essential to find projects the company cares about, and to speak directly with an employee that can become an internal champion. Most contracts end up signed by a C-level employee, which means that there is a long chain you have to survive without being there to champion yourself. It goes a long way to have a solution to a problem they are already looking to solve, otherwise you can get stuck in dead ends that drag out.

In my experience, companies that vacillate when it's time to start drafting an agreement rarely move forward at that time. That being said, we've had several companies re-approach us months or years later. This shows the importance of developing good relationships and a strong reputation. While many companies may not be ready to jump on opportunities immediately, and may string you along as they figure that out, they will be ready someday. It's important to be top-of-mind when that happens.

In areas where there is high turnover of employees, maintaining these networks and relationships can be especially challenging.

How long does an enterprise deal typically take you to close, from start to finish?

The time from first contact to a signed agreement is usually about six to nine months. From there, contracts range from months to years.

How do you maintain a strong relationship with your corporate partner once the deal has been closed?

This is a challenge for small companies, especially as turnover can be high at larger organizations. Our approach is to continually search for new opportunities which leverage our partners in a mutually beneficial way. This could mean connecting them to other partners or projects in our network, or exploring ways to expand or improve completed projects. The best way to maintain a strong relationship is to continue adding value.

We also check in periodically over email, and try to use any mutual events as an opportunity to catch up more personally.

Is there anything you wish corporate innovators knew about startups that would improve your interactions?

The hardest part of working with a large company, for startups, is that the timetables are extremely long. Small companies often do not have the resources to develop robust sales pipelines and portfolios of leads, which means that many can bleed out waiting on large first contracts to hit. I'm not sure if corporate partners always realize that this is a real constraint for small companies and startups.

In many ways, startups operate more like a private contractor than a large corporation. Every project they undertake is critical to cash flow, and they schedule very tightly to meet those opportunities they see as best. Working with large companies involves inevitable delays as project teams try to secure all the approvals and inputs associated with safely bringing new products to market. If companies understood the extent to which this can bleed out a smaller company, there might be room to streamline the process, in turn providing more security to startups, likely lowering prices and improving rates of success.

Additionally, I think some large corporations have a tendency to undervalue input from startups. Since they have more resources and experience, many seem overly confident of tackling new challenges in-house, when there is almost always some startup that has already been living this new market for years. I believe we need a shift in focus from ignoring, competing, then buying startups, to nurturing and partnering with them from the beginning. By doing so, both startups and large companies can focus on the areas they know best, find the right solutions to large problems, and then scale those solutions very quickly. This is not to say corporations shouldn't cherry-pick the best solutions to work with, only that they should do it sooner in the process and take a more active role in supporting the transition to scale.

What is the most important thing you've learned about startup-corporate interactions since becoming a founder?

I've learned how important it is for startup technology to fit into industry trends. With the right startup-corporate partnership, new technology can be brought to market at an incredible pace. Startups bring experiences in the trenches, building solutions that no corporation can match. Corporations bring the resources and the market reach to grow the right solutions to scale. However, many companies are understandably very careful with these resources, and can at times be very careless with a startup. I don't think it's malicious, just a misunderstanding of the way constraints and limited resources affect startup sales processes. At the end of the day, if a large company is not fired up about moving forward, as a startup it's usually better to focus elsewhere while maintaining a friendly relationship. As the startup grows and builds the resources to manage a broader pipeline, they can then look to expand their pipeline down the line. If you're not in line with the collective momentum of the industry, it becomes an uphill battle very quickly.

To learn more about Arden and PieceMaker Technologies' groundbreaking work in 3D printing, please visit www.piece-maker.com.

Interview with Bill Belias, Founder of Ergonex

What is the counterargument to the "It's never worthwhile using consultants" argument?

The interesting thing is that consultants are often thought of as experts, but I don't think that's necessarily the main reason that would make a consultant effective. I believe that a consultant has the ability to focus on a problem without the noise that's found in a company. A company usually has a number of—let's say fifty—people who are all involved in a given project. And they're never involved full-time, they're just in and out. Whereas a consultant who is brought in to work on a problem looks at it differently. They are able to focus. It's like bringing in a computer that's brought in to focus on one algorithm as opposed to a server that's working on many different programs at once.

Within companies, there's this sense that when they bring in a consultant, that person needs to be an expert. Little do they realize that learning to be an expert is a skill. And that skill happens to be something that consultants are often good at.

Consultants also have less fear—which is important for innovation. There are many types of fear, such as "my boss is going to think I'm stupid" or "if I make a mistake, I'll get fired." With employees, people often prioritize their own promotions over the task at hand. Whereas a consultant knows that there is never a promotion coming to them, so they are much more focused on the task at hand.

How does compensation structure tie into the effectiveness of a consultant?

Compensation based on results—i.e., successfully solving the problem results in a certain amount of money—I think would be better. In general, however, people are hesitant to go down that route. I have suggested results-based compensation in many companies, including some of my customers, and many of them don't like that. Because they aren't used to it. And part of it is because they themselves are paid whether or not they solve the problem. So they would rather keep things simple and what they're used to.

Results-based compensation can also be risky from a company's perspective because at the end of the project, the consultant could choose to say that they didn't successfully complete the project, not get paid, and then ultimately turn around and sell the results to a competitor. So there's a risk there also that companies, particularly large ones, are solving for.

Tell me a bit about the startup side of the work that you do.

I've gotten involved with a lot of startups over the years. And generally startups don't have a lot of money. They're kind of working in what I call "starvation mode." But I usually like the problems startups are trying to solve, and I spend about a quarter of my time with startups. Usually when I go in, I try to solve whatever problem they're looking for help on in exchange for equity. Sometimes startups have raised significant funding, so they'd rather just pay me for my services in cash; but in general I ask for equity instead of cash when working with startups.

The positive reason to spend a lot of time with startups is because they're more dynamic, they are closer to the customer, and you learn a lot about new-business development. It's an education, and there are a lot of good things that startups can teach you.

Do you have any examples of when you've connected startups and large companies?

One of my startup clients is a sustainable packaging company called Sweetwater. I've been connecting them with companies like Procter & Gamble, Nestle, and Pepsi, who are all searching for sustainable packaging solutions. Sweetwater's technology is unique and brings strong value to any large company they work with.

Startups often understand their world—the technology or product. But what's often missing is the connections and mind-set that allows them to work with large companies, particularly large companies who are directly connected to the consumer. This is where I can provide value to startup clients.

What are some things you wish startups knew about how large companies operate on the inside?

Large companies are slow . . . but methodical. With lots of processes . . . and red tape. If you haven't spent time in both startups and large companies, it's extremely difficult to connect the two and understand how to bridge the gap. At some point in the startup life cycle, whether it's as a customer, retailer, or something, you are going to be dependent on large companies. And you need to be able to manage your own expectations—know that you're going to be fighting a battle for possibly even two years. And you need to manage your funding with that time line in mind.

What are some things you wish large companies knew about how to work with startups?

I always make my big-company clients aware that startups are nimble; they have quick ways to test business models. Large companies should all devote a certain amount of time and re-sources to startup situations, whether that is working with ex-isting startups or starting and spinning out their own. P&G is a company using this model well.

Interview with Brian Ardinger, Founder of the Inside/Outside Innovation Summit, Inside/Outside Innovation Podcast, Econic, and nMotion Accelerator

Tell me about the inspiration behind the Inside/Outside Innovation Summit and the podcast.

The [Inside/Outside Innovation] podcast's original inspiration was to look at tech startups outside the Valley. Then it morphed into talking to innovators inside and outside large companies. The conference came by us noticing that there's a real need to bring people from the two different backgrounds—startup and corporate—into the same room. We wanted to see what would happen when you bring the "ties and the T-shirts" together.

Part of our goal with the conference is to scare the pants off corporate and show them the scale of innovation taking place. The days of a business model lasting fifty years are gone. So we try to give companies the context of innovation and exposure to startups who are building new things. It provides perspective. Seeing a two-person team being able to spin something up gives you a different outlook and shows you what's really possible.

Who attends the Inside/Outside Innovation Summit from the corporate side?

We try to find corporate innovators that are already attempting to be more innovative—for example, people who are trying to use lean startup methodology or innovators running their own accelerator or lab. This ensures that the connections are relevant for everyone involved.

How do you help large companies create a strategy for how to work with startups? Do you have any examples you can point to?

Often, we work with companies who are already looking at the startups in their space (for example, insurance firms looking at insurance tech); but there are usually wider, tangential opportunities that are relevant for the large company, which they're missing. So we often advise companies on how to cast a wider net for the types of startups they are looking at.

One example that immediately comes to mind is BMW in Europe. They created an accelerator that worked quite a bit differently from other corporate accelerators. They looked for startups with interesting technology and brought them into this accelerated vendor pipeline, which allowed BMW to quickly become a customer. This was nontraditional because they weren't investing in startups for equity, but instead it was built around how to get technology into their company early and easily.

Can taking money from a corporate venture capital group be risky?

It depends on the industry. If you're in an industry with only a couple major players where if you start working with one, you are "tainted" for the others, that's a risk. In other situations, if there's only one logical acquirer anyway, it might not be very risky to start working together early.

What is something you wish corporates knew about startups?

I always wish they understood how fast and furious the startup side is and how any delay can really have a big effect on a startup. I wish they would recognize that any time you engage with a startup, you are taking them off their game. Understand that taking two or three weeks to schedule a meeting is normal pace on the corporate side but is a huge deal on the startup side. Respecting the speed at which a startup has to move to basically maintain its life is oftentimes overlooked, especially if the corporate person has never been in a startup.

What is something you wish startups knew about corporates?

I've noticed that the startups that are good at working with corporates tend to be ones with founders who have worked on the corporate side. Sometimes startups can get cocky about disrupting the industry, etc., etc. Don't get cocky about things, and really work to find your advocate within your target corporate partner.

To learn more about the Inside/Outside Innovation Summit, please visit www.theiosummit.com

Interview with Dave Knox, Founder of the Brandery, CMO of Rockfish (Acquired by WPP), Author of *Predicting the Turn: The High Stakes Game of Business Between Startups and Blue Chips*

In your opinion, what are the pros and cons for startups considering taking corporate venture capital?

I see an almost equal number of pros and cons for taking corporate venture capital. So if I were a startup, I would ask myself why the corporate is getting involved and what stage they typically get involved at.

It's really important to look at the potential downside, too. This can happen if the company is just too early or, alternatively, if the large company's competitors won't engage with you simply because you have taken an investment from one of their rivals. That could make things really tricky very fast.

It's really easy to see all the positives of working with a large corporate partner; but as the CEO, it's important to pay attention to the downside also.

Are there any particularly good examples you've seen personally of large companies and startups working together for mutual benefit?

A really good example of a deal where there was a win-win on both sides is when Caterpillar invested in (and later acquired) Yard Club. For Yard Club, the investment didn't really cut them off from any future options with other companies in the industry. Meanwhile, Caterpillar was able to explore and study this peer-to-peer lending model to see if there was any merit to it before making a big bet.

The TechStars Disney program is particularly interesting to me. We had one of our Brandery companies go through their accelerator—the company is FamilyTech. The company had already raised a Series A and about half the companies in the accelerator had raised a Series A or beyond—so clearly not a typical accelerator. Our company came into the accelerator with the clear goal that they wanted to collaborate. One of the tangible things that came out of that collaboration was the BB8 Robot, which a couple years ago was Disney's top-selling holiday toy. That's what can happen when these collaborations are done right.

What are some pitfalls you've seen startups fall into when trying to work with large companies?

There are a lot of respected VCs that tell their companies to avoid engaging with large companies, especially early on. The first reason for that is when you see the potential of the deal size, you put all your eggs in one basket and the founder is so focused on getting that deal done. And we know that these deals take a long time within corporate, and there are a lot of factors that go into that. A founder can waste so much time, money, and effort to get that deal done and can wake up one day and be out of money.

The second issue is treating your enterprise customer as the most important customer, especially when it comes to product feedback. This can effectively turn you into a product development shop for your corporate partner and stunt your growth.

Is there anything you wish founders knew about working with large companies—whether selling to them, partnering, or being acquired?

You as a startup are going to move incredibly fast, because you have a burn rate. Your conversation with your corporate counterpart is probably your most important conversation of the day. Conversely, for the person in corporate, their conversation with you is highly unlikely to be their most important conversation of the day.

You as a startup founder can typically make decisions as you want. Meanwhile, in the large company there are checks and balances which require buy-in from multiple stakeholders. So that means your internal champion is probably fighting hard on your behalf, but that there is a process for them to go through that may require approval from four, five, or six different people. Being cognizant of that and doing what you can to make your champion's life easier can be powerful. But you need to be patient.

Can you elaborate on the pain point startups are solving for large companies today?

Startups are, in many ways, the canary in the coal mine for big companies today. They can be the warning system for changes that are taking place in the marketplace. It's a really interesting thing for a large company to be able to engage with a startup and see how they are impacting and changing the industry, before it has even played out. It's hugely valuable. You could almost argue that startups are the new R&D for large companies.

What is the risk for founders who outsource their corporate/sales partnerships?

There is a risk of working with a completely outsourced service which works as outsourced business development. While these companies can be great for opening up doors, by removing yourself (as the founder) from the conversation, you no longer have access to the ideas and product feedback that these companies might be able to provide.

The better approach to outsourcing would be to find someone or a company that will open up doors for you but still include you in the conversations so that you aren't cutting yourself off from the feedback you need to improve your product.

I would also advise founders to be careful as they evaluate outside firms and make sure that the firm (or at least the group you're working with) isn't getting paid on both the corporate and startup sides. Aligning incentives is key.

To learn more about Dave's book and work, please visit www. predictingtheturn.com.

Interview with Chaz Giles, Head of Global External Innovation at Estée Lauder, Founder at MomTrusted.com, Former Director at Citi Ventures, and Former Manager at Procter & Gamble's FutureWorks

Chaz has spent significant time on all sides of the startup-corporate ecosystem. While at P&G, he helped to spin up and run Future-Works, an innovation group focused on new business model development. He then spent time at Citi Ventures, where he made investments across a variety of industries and regions. From there, he went on to start MomTrusted.com, a digital marketplace that leverages the social graph to help parents find trusted childcare options. And finally he launched and now runs Global External Innovation at The Estée Lauder Companies. Quite a résumé, and of course he had quite a lot to share in our interview.

What is the biggest challenge for corporate innovators?

Most corporate innovators are judged on dual success metrics: financial and strategic. Financial is, in many ways, the simpler and more straightforward goal. Strategic goals are a lot tougher to achieve for corporate innovators and investment groups.

Assumptions built around strategic value can be really tricky. Oftentimes, there is a group executing the deal (for example a venture group) and the strategic value being built into the value of the deal is coming from a specific business unit. There is a lot behind those assumptions—they require input from operational teams, they require a steady direction for the overall company for a certain period of time, and they potentially require new capabilities to be built to achieve that value.

For example, when tech companies make acquisitions, they typically buy companies within their core competency. A search company buying an ad-pricing algorithm, for example. However, outside of tech, most acquisitions are made with the intent of moving the acquiring company into a new type of business. This requires new capabilities to be built to realize that value—which are easy to draft on paper, but a lot harder to execute in real life. These integrations are challenging and super-tricky to get right.

How should founders think about the deal funnel that their corporate counterpart is dealing with, and how can they make sure their deal is prioritized?

As a founder, your world is literal and direct. The only reason your company works is because every morning, you and your team show up and make the company move. With larger companies, they have the inertia in-market that continues to drive them, so there is a different sense of urgency on their side. It's not good or bad, it just simply is. Depending on which side of the table you're on, you have to either speed up the urgency or pace your team a bit more.

Founders also need to understand that within companies there are cascading sets of priorities. There are the overall company's priorities, there are the business-unit priorities, there are brand strategies/priorities, regional strategies and priorities, etc., etc. This is very different than startups, where there is essentially one priority. So what startups need to understand is that when they are dealing with someone within a large company, they are dealing with someone who is somewhere in that ladder of priorities, and their job as an early-stage company is *not* to convince this person that their technology is the greatest thing ever: their job is to figure out how to hook their goals into that ladder of priorities at that bigger company. The more they can work to understand each of those priority sets, the more the deal will come together.

Are there best practices or tactics that founders can use to make their corporate counterparts' lives easier?

I'm still surprised at how many founders keep conversations in sales mode instead of progressing them to strategic-partner mode. Obviously, at the beginning you're selling—you need to get in the door. But once you have a receptive conversation, the ratio of speaking versus listening needs to change dramatically. The goal at that point is about listening to that organization and understanding the itches, the pain points—and hooking your solution to those itches and pain points.

In startups, the KPIs (Key Performance Indicators) and goals are usually somewhat straightforward. When dealing with large organizations, these things are not at all obvious. There can be nuances that affect what someone gets their bonus for. For example, if I'm given a bonus for streamlining procurement and you're a startup selling in and complicating things, that means that you are literally moving my key metric in the wrong direction—even if the startup is very, very valuable.

This can show up in a variety of other ways, too. For example, contract structure: a company may be trying to reduce their recurring costs. So by structuring your contract with a lower recurring cost but a higher success fee, you may be increasing the overall cost of the deal, but the *individual* you are dealing with doesn't care about overall cost: they only care about recurring cost. But you would only know that by listening and understanding what people are measured on and rewarded for.

How do you build a great relationship with founders before, during, and after the deal process?

A lot of it starts with me having had a shared experience with them—I know what they are going through. Something that I think a lot of people in corporate miss is that, for founders and team members, their startup is more than just a job. This is something they have poured their heart, their soul, and potentially their savings into. It is truly personal for them. There is no such thing as "it's just business, not personal" when you're in startup world. Understanding this would go a long way toward helping folks on the corporate side understand why people on the startup side act and react the way that they do.

Corporate folks also need to understand that "no" is an okay response. In dealing with small companies, it is not about keeping hope alive: it's about being super-transparent. If a partnership could work and there is something to be had, of course say that. But if it doesn't work and you don't think it will go anywhere, then say that as well. That level of transparency is refreshing and welcome as a founder. Founders use this feedback to choose where to deploy their time and resources. Not being transparent with your feedback doesn't allow them to do this in an effective manner.

Is there anything you wish startups knew about large companies?

The biggest thing is that literally everything is different. The time horizons are different, the metrics are different, the priorities are different. It's all different.

This means you need to understand all of this and plan for it. That could mean a different sales strategy or even a different fund-raising strategy. You could do things like partner with an existing vendor so you can avoid the procurement process, etc.

But most importantly, you need to study how large companies interact and operate.

Is there anything you wish corporate innovators knew about startups?

Corporate innovators need to understand the speed at which startups move and, because of that, the need for clarity. If you respect those things and are clear and transparent with what you can and can't do, you'll have some great interactions. Similarly, make sure you follow up. Too many times, there are great meetings that large companies have with small ones, but then priorities change and things happen without any follow-up. I really think this is where reputations are won and lost, for large companies among startups.

For example, by being clear and precise on why you aren't moving forward, the startup can incorporate that feedback and iterate, so that in four to six months when they come back, now they've helped you solve your problem and you're eager to engage with them. But that iteration can only happen if you are clear and brutally honest with feedback.

In addition, I think large organizations need to have translators (people who have been on both sides of the ecosystem) who can help to cut through the language, so to speak. Oftentimes, there's an unmet need in translating between what large companies are saying and what startups are saying.

Finally, large companies should consider putting together an "innovation execution" function. As I said earlier, on paper an innovation opportunity might make sense; but to actually go execute, today that falls to the business units, who are often already running at full capacity. So having other teams and groups who can implement pilots, build new functions, and create connections between brand and technology. This would change conversations with business units from a hypothetical business impact to "this technology led to an X% lift in revenue during the pilot." Things become much more tangible, and it is easier to know how to prioritize and invest.

Interview with Nim De Swardt, Chief Next Generation Officer at Bacardi

Tell me about your experience as a corporate innovator.

Working at Bacardi as Chief Next Generation Officer is a dream Intrapreneur framework. In partnership with Michael Dolan, the Bacardi CEO, together we are armed with a bold vision and brave moves. Our mission is to ensure Bacardi is ahead of the game as they prepare for the future of work.

My role is one of influence, not power. It is my duty to elevate and inspire the Next Generation of leaders, showcase the great potential of internal innovation, forge new external partnerships while managing a groundbreaking intrapreneurship program across twenty countries and seventeen internal functions.

NEXT GEN is a cultural driver of relevancy and future thinking. We constructively disrupt the corporate beast DNA through taking risks to make epic shit happen. We are playing the long game, developing a global NEXT GEN strategy for Bacardi's 6,500-strong workforce that will ensure a 154-year company lives on sustainably.

Great change can come from within corporates. Through NEXT GEN we are massaging the behavior and traditional thinking of the corporate system to adapt to the rapidly changing consumer and employee demands. The secret sauce? A powerful partnership cemented in trust and transparency. The Architect, Michael Dolan, a future-thinking CEO; and me, a hyper-curious passionate millennial acting as the "Activator" or "Composer."

Individuality beats conventionality. It's okay to be an outlier in a large organization if you are 100 percent purpose-driven. As a corporate innovator, you need to understand what game you are in and if you truly want to play it. If the path is clear, you are probably on the wrong path. My inspiration and drive is personal: activating entrepreneurial spirits in people and employees fulfills and thrills me. We have seen firsthand through NEXT GEN the great power of culture change through community in corporates, aligned on our mission of #bettertogether.

Show up and own it. The best piece of advice a female executive mentor ever gave me. Being the youngest direct report to a Global CEO and not being connected to any department cements my role in disruption. I rose to this occasion through my personal values, a wicked foundational combination of courage, passion, resilience, and empathy. Being an Intrapreneur cemented my belief in the "Cs" of life: chance, change, courage, curiosity, culture, community, creativity, and compassion.

You have to have faith in your capabilities to embrace constant change as an Intrapreneur. Business changes, leadership changes, societal changes, the changing consumer—unknown over known, wild over tame, change over constant, courage over comfort.

Corporate C Suites around the world face similar challenges. "Everything is all good" is a message that is constantly being projected to the top. What if we delivered honest introspection, front-line employee insights, and reframe our biggest challenges as our greatest opportunity? The new world of business and work needs to accept they are now balancing a fine line between traditions and driving a new world change agenda.

This job is a journey in a room of funhouse mirrors that constantly delivers huge introspection. I am exposed to hundreds of employee journeys, emotions, challenges, trials, tribulations, and celebrations on a daily basis. It is like observing the natural circle of life—the internal action and reactions. My secret strategy? "Win from within"—encouraging them to look inside themselves. There is a great mirror in the inner life as a leader, the actions they take, the impact they make, the relationships they build—you need to first understand what is going on inside you before you can navigate the noises around you. Psychological safety—it's what we all crave, so why is it so feared in the corporate world? When you are exposed to so many parallels of diversity—backgrounds, perspectives, cultures, functions, age— it makes you realize we are all really just human. And humanity is what we crave more than ever. Building a human-centric culture with priorities on building trust, breaking down hierarchy barriers, encouraging peer-to-peer support and feedback, driving recognition, and encouraging freedom of thought activates the right purpose, making work joyful and pushing employees to yield innovative results.

Human-centric leadership can be chaotic at times. We are all emotionally and mentally made up differently, but our cores are all the same. I see the best Intrapreneurs constantly striving to foster innovation through collaboration, to drive motivation and productivity without the hierarchy and power-tripping authority in their companies. But most of all, I see them being empathic— to themselves and to others through the priority of "Winning from Within."

How do you and your team measure success? Do you have any examples or recommendations?

Give away ownership. Success is a team sport. Trust the timing of your life. Success from a corporate innovator's perspective can be based as much on ROR (Return On Relationships) as ROI (Return On Investment). We closed an Enterprise partnership with WeWork at their new Mexico City co-working hub, securing eighty desks for Bacardi Mexico employees. This was a huge step for Bacardi toward the future of work and future employee. Good-bye traditional office cubicles, hello fresh future of work space and invigorating environment. External partnerships are powerful, and new-world collaboration is a key sustainability thread for large corporates. Collaboration, cooperation, and co-creation—the Cs of partnership.

NextGen feels like an epic social experiment—a constant cross-sectional journey of cultures, functions, and generations. My role is to "get under the hood" of an organization: real culture starts from the individual level, not from the top. We are "getting it bubbling up" by empowering future Next Generation leaders to be change agents, the change they want to see. Managing up, managing down, mentoring up, mentoring around—this is not a game of power plays. It is my personal commitment to the great future of our Next Generation leaders at Bacardi. I am in a unique position of influence to spark and generate shared purpose to all employees in inclusive ways. My Intrapreneur role sets me "out of the hierarchy"—at the center of an epic circle of possibility and positivity, not the top of the pyramid. You have to be bold and brave. Sell your vision first—business and people impact included. Go with your gut—take risks—comfort is no norm as an Intrapreneur. "On the fly"—Mike always reminds me to stay flexible and responsive, sometimes change agent navigation tests you—mentally and emotionally. Always go back to your core values—these are your cement and will drive you daily.

You are you. Never forget this. You are not your job title, who you report to, or what you have accomplished—you are YOU. As an Intrapreneur, I have been reminded daily of who I am and the power of great charismatic energy that radiates to others. As a leader I have been graced with so many opportunities to spark energy and imagination in employees all over the world; this is the true fuel to my internal fire. It is the ability to influence authentically through personal relationships that sets the right foundations to produce the results, foster collective ownership, and empower others to have the persistence and belief in the core vision of possibility. If you are brave enough to push the institutional frameworks as an Intrapreneur, you have to firstly drive only what you believe in, secondly never forget your core values, and third but most importantly—self-awareness—you know who you are.

When approaching a startup or external organization, what does your process look like?

My motto is "Make moves where you can make waves." There is no process. You identify an opportunity, potential partnership, or startup of interest, and you think, "Could this actually eventuate into something special for both parties?" If the passion and belief isn't in your blood, don't do it. Corporate innovators lack process and are masters of fluid moves. We know that diversity powers broader thinking, and we are brave enough to constantly infuse that diverse thinking into the organization where we face the ongoing resistance for anything "new" or "out of priority." Be strategic and pick your battles, get ready to embark on a cluttered path, get ready to get quiet and feel like an outlier. Most approaches begin with a relationship, forming a common intention and then embarking on a rapidly fast or painstakingly slow process called a "partnership." The thing is, there is great beauty in the corporate-startup partnership process because it's almost like you take the most analytical minds and put them in front of a blank canvas with a rainbow of paints. It makes them flex muscles they don't often flex, without the usual structure and ball-breaking hierarchy.

To learn more about Nim and her work, please visit www.nim-deswardt.com.

APPENDIX 2

CORPORATE INNOVATION SCORECARD EXAMPLE

When corporate innovators are evaluating potential companies to work with, they often use a scorecard. This allows them to add some quantitative definition to a decision that they'll need to defend down the line. There are multiple categories, each with a few parameters.

Strategic Fit

Does it link to a core "Where to Play" area?
(*Yes = 4, No = 0*)

Does it create a breakthrough or new category (aka disruptive or WOW factor)? (*Yes = 4, No = 0*)

Should this be done externally? (*Yes = 4, No = 0*)

Technical Feasibility

Is this project technically feasible? (*Yes = 4, No = 0*)

Can this technology give us results higher than our current benchmark? (*Yes = 4, No = 0*)

Safety, Regulatory, and Legal Risks

Is there a safety risk? (*Low = 5, Medium = 3, High = 1*)

Is there a legal risk? (*Low = 3, Medium = 2, High = 1*)

Is there a regulatory risk? (*Low = 3, Medium = 2, High = 1*)

Intellectual Property Potential

Can we create IP? (*Yes = 3, No = 0*)

Do we need a freedom to operate search? (*No = 2, Yes = 0*)

Estimated Time to Market

How long will this take to put into market?
(*0–12 months = 3, 12–24 months = 2, 24+ months = 1*)

Strength of Partner

How well funded is the partner?
(*Well funded = 2, Not well funded = 0*)

How strong is the partner's technical team?
(*Strong = 2, Not strong = 0*)

Each project in the portfolio is given a score and then prioritized. While these scores are obviously not perfect descriptors of each individual project, having some type of quantified score allows internal discussion and comparison of projects.

For startups, it's important to know that these are the metrics by which you are being judged, at least at the beginning. Startups would be well served to take these parameters into account as they plan their pitch and how to best position their technology or service.

NOTES

Chapter 1

1. A term coined by entrepreneur Steve Blank, meaning activities that are designed to appear innovative but aren't. Common examples: innovation field trips, Silicon Valley "outposts," and adding the word "innovation" to people's titles without changing their job function.
2. To be fair, it's only in hindsight that the Internet is so obviously a game changer for every industry.
3. You can also make the case that DVDs were essential to Netflix's early success. VHS tapes would have been too expensive to mail and Blockbuster's DVD selection was a point of weakness.
4. For those too young to remember, Blockbuster required you to rewind VHS movies before returning them to avoid a fine.
5. A good rule of thumb in business: never underestimate humanity's laziness. Laziness, not necessity, is the true mother of invention.
6. Coined by Harvard Business School professor Clayton Christensen in 1997.
7. https://lens.blogs.nytimes.com/2015/08/12/kodaks-first-digital-moment/.
8. Kids, if this sounds like a foreign language to you, that's okay. Basically, this is how pictures were taken back in the day.

Chapter 2

1. Business-school kids: don't quote me on that definition.
2. Spoiler alert: it won't be.
3. The organization chart (aka org chart) is a visual representation of the corporate hierarchy.

Chapter 3

1. Though your odds may actually be higher in *The Hunger Games*.
2. We'll call it the Meeting Scheduling Postulate.

3. Unfortunately, this is when you'll find a lot of calendar availability.
4. A word to wise corporate employees: get good at passively listening while typing/doing other work. You'll seem engaged in the call and still get lots of work done. People will admire your productivity and jokingly say things like, "You must have a clone." That's a good thing.
5. This tactic will not surprise anyone in startup world.
6. https://techcrunch.com/2012/02/01/facebook-ipo-letter/.

Chapter 6

1. Later, we'll look at how corporate innovators sometimes screw up and what you can do to prevent and correct for those mistakes.

Chapter 7

1. https://medium.com/startups-and-investment/the-pros-and-cons-of-taking-investment-from-corporate-vcs-b8164023a938.

Chapter 8

1. In this case, "global" refers to all regions *and* all industries. It is not used just to describe geography.

Chapter 9

1. Corporate innovators reading this: definitely use this tactic if you can manage it.
2. Shout-out to Kanye.

INDEX